VIBE DEEP

VIBE DEEP

A.J. SOLANO

CONTENTS

Let's be real—finding out who you are can feel like searching for a signal in a world that's always "on." With constant updates, posts, and filters, it's easy to get caught up in what we *think* we should be. But what if I told you that somewhere beneath all of that, there's a more powerful, unfiltered version of you? That's the vibe we're after here. It's not about creating a new you or living up to anyone's standards; it's about uncovering who you already are.

Welcome to a journey of authenticity, where self-acceptance and self-discovery become your guideposts. Why now? Because the world around us has only gotten louder and the pressure to "fit in" has intensified. So many of us are left wondering if we're enough, as we scroll through highlight reels and try to keep up with everyone else's version of success. But here's a truth worth holding onto: You *are* enough, right here, just as you are.

In this book, we're tuning out that noise together and getting back to what's real. We'll dive into self-awareness, understanding your core values, and learning to trust yourself without needing validation from anyone else. This isn't about achieving some perfect version of yourself. It's about stepping into your life with a sense of clarity, kindness, and confidence that comes from truly knowing yourself. The deeper you go, the more powerful you'll feel in your own skin—and in a world full of filters, *that's* the real flex.

So, take a deep breath. This is your space, your time. This is where you get to just *be*, where no one's expectations define you. Together, we'll explore what it means to live in a way that's true to *you* and feels good from the inside out. Whether you're looking for a sense of purpose, peace, or just a break from the constant noise, let this book be your guide to vibing deeply with who you are, exactly as you are.

Let's get into it.

Tuning Out the Noise

Why Disconnecting Matters

With notifications buzzing and timelines constantly updating, it's easy to lose yourself in the endless scroll. Social media, streaming, and online culture bring us closer to the world, but they can also create a kind of digital haze, making it harder to see where you truly stand. Have you ever felt a low hum of anxiety after hours on your phone? Or felt a dip in confidence after seeing everyone else's "perfect" lives? That's the impact of digital noise—it can blur your sense of self-worth and leave you feeling drained, even when you're surrounded by the latest and greatest in entertainment and connectivity.

Taking a step back isn't about saying goodbye to your devices. It's about giving yourself space to breathe, think, and just *be* without constantly needing to check in. Disconnecting lets you reconnect with your inner voice, hear your own thoughts more clearly, and gain a fresh perspective on what genuinely matters to you.

How to Begin

Creating mindful space in a hyper-connected world might feel tricky, but small changes can make a big difference. Here are some gentle ways to start disconnecting, just a little, each day:

1. **Designate "Device-Free" Zones**: Pick a few times or places—like meals, mornings, or bedtime—where you put your phone away entirely. Without that constant urge to check, you'll find space for stillness.

2. **Limit Notifications**: Most notifications are designed to pull you back in. Try turning off non-essential notifications or using "Do Not Disturb" mode during study sessions or when you're spending time with loved ones.

3. **Set Screen Time Goals**: Challenge yourself with realistic goals—like cutting back by 10% each week. Track your progress and notice any shifts in your mood or energy.

4. **Engage in One Offline Activity Daily**: Spend at least 10-15 minutes doing something away from screens. It could be journaling, taking a walk, cooking, or even daydreaming—anything that reconnects you to your own rhythm.

5. **Practice "Single-Tasking"**: Multitasking can lead to feeling scattered. Try focusing on one thing at a time, whether it's reading a book, listening to music, or having a conversation. Being fully present can be surprisingly grounding.

Weekly Exercise: The Digital Cleanse

Take a day this week for a mini "digital cleanse." Here's a step-by-step guide:

1. **Pick Your Day**: Choose a day you feel you can manage without checking your phone or computer constantly—maybe it's Sunday or even just an evening during the week.

2. **Prepare Ahead**: Let friends or family know you'll be offline for the day or a few hours, so there's no pressure to respond quickly.

3. **Set Intentions**: Before you start, write down one or two intentions for the day. Maybe you want to relax, reflect, or do some-

thing creative. This gives you a purpose and keeps you grounded as you disconnect.

4.   **Plan Simple Activities**: Make a list of things you enjoy that don't require screens—whether it's going for a walk, baking, reading, or organizing something in your room.

5.   **Reflect**: At the end of your cleanse, take a moment to reflect. Did you feel different? Did you feel calmer, more focused, or even a bit restless? Noticing these emotions can help you better understand the role of digital noise in your life.

Try repeating this exercise weekly, extending the amount of time if it feels right. Over time, you'll start to notice patterns—both in how you respond to being offline and in the way you reconnect with yourself when you're not tuned into the digital world.

Final Thought

The online world will always be there, but these moments of quiet reflection are your opportunity to recharge. When you give yourself even a small break from digital noise, you make room for your own thoughts and feelings, which strengthens your connection to yourself. Disconnecting doesn't mean you're missing out; it means you're choosing to tune in to what really matters. Remember, it's not about cutting ties with the digital world altogether but about finding the balance that feels right for you.

So start small, notice the difference, and let this be a gentle reminder: the most important connection you'll ever make is the one with yourself.

CHAPTER 2

Beyond the Likes

In the world of social media, a double-tap or a comment can feel like a small but powerful burst of validation. Each like, share, or follow can feel like a little reminder that people see you, that they appreciate you, that you're valued. But here's the tricky part: when we rely too much on external validation, especially from social media, we start to build our confidence on something that's always shifting and never fully in our control. It becomes easy to start seeing ourselves through the eyes of others rather than through our own.

Learning to separate validation from social media means shifting that source of worth inward, so you're not constantly checking a feed to feel "enough." This doesn't mean you can't enjoy the thrill of a like or a positive comment; it just means you'll have a solid foundation of self-worth that doesn't depend on it. Reclaiming inner confidence is about recognizing that your value exists regardless of whether it's acknowledged online.

How to Reclaim Inner Confidence

To start building inner confidence and reducing the need for social validation, try these steps:

1. **Ask "Who Am I Without the Likes?"**
When you strip away the audience, the filters, and the curated posts, who are you? Take some time to reflect on what you love about yourself, even if no one else sees it. Knowing what makes you *you* can strengthen that inner sense of value.

2. **Stop Linking Self-Worth to Numbers**
Try to detach your self-worth from numbers like likes, followers, and comments. If you find yourself feeling down after a post doesn't "perform," remind yourself that a number doesn't define the quality of who you are. Think of it as feedback for the algorithm—not for you.

3. **Celebrate Efforts, Not Outcomes**
Instead of focusing on how many people liked your post, focus on what made you want to share it in the first place. Celebrate the creative act of expressing yourself, regardless of how it's received. Confidence grows when you're proud of your effort, not just the reaction.

4. **Practice Self-Validation**
Before you look to others for validation, practice affirming yourself. Look in the mirror, give yourself a compliment, or remind yourself of a recent achievement, big or small. Self-validation is a habit, and like all habits, it gets stronger with practice.

5. **Limit "Compare and Despair" Scrolling**
It's easy to fall into comparison mode when scrolling. If you find yourself constantly comparing, set boundaries on your social media use, like limiting it to certain times of day or unfollowing accounts that trigger self-doubt. Curating a positive feed can help you enjoy social media without losing sight of your own journey.

Weekly Exercise: Confidence Journaling

This week, try a confidence journaling exercise to build self-assurance from the inside out.

1. **Daily Gratitude for You**

   Each night, write down three things you appreciate about yourself. They don't have to be huge—maybe it's the way you handled a conversation, the effort you put into a project, or a quality you admire in yourself, like kindness or resilience.

2. **Personal "Highlight Reel"**

   List a few moments you're proud of that don't involve social media. Maybe it's a small win at school, a hobby you enjoy, a supportive friend you're grateful for, or a risk you took. Reminding yourself of these moments regularly reinforces your confidence outside of the digital world.

3. **Track Your Mood**

   If you find yourself reaching for your phone to check social media, pause and take a quick inventory of how you feel. Are you bored, lonely, or looking for a distraction? Noticing these moments will help you become more aware of when you're seeking validation and why.

4. **Check in at Week's End**

   At the end of the week, read over your journal entries. Reflect on any positive shifts in your mood or self-perception. This habit helps build confidence from within and reduces the urge to seek constant approval from others.

Final Thought

Validation from others can feel good, but the most lasting confidence comes from within. Social media can reflect parts of who you are, but it's not the whole picture—and it never has to be. Your worth doesn't fluctuate with the number of likes, followers, or comments you receive. When you shift the focus inward, you'll find a confidence that's not only steady but powerful.

Remember, there's something special about knowing your own value without needing anyone else to tell you. As you go through this journey, remind yourself often: your value is real, it's constant, and it's not defined by a screen. Embrace it, hold onto it, and know that you are more than enough just as you are.

CHAPTER 3

Why We Compare

It's natural to compare yourself to others; we've all done it. From grades to career paths, social circles to social media feeds, it's easy to look at someone else's life and wonder if you're measuring up. But here's the truth: comparison can be a thief of joy, making us question our worth and redirecting our focus away from our own growth. When we constantly measure ourselves against others, we often lose sight of the unique qualities and achievements that make us who we are.

The comparison trap keeps you looking outward, but real self-discovery happens when you start looking inward. This chapter is about shifting from "How do I measure up?" to "How can I build on my strengths?" It's about recognizing that your path doesn't have to look like anyone else's—and, in fact, it *shouldn't*.

How to Escape the Comparison Trap

Breaking the habit of comparison takes practice, but these steps can help you center yourself on your own unique journey:

1. **Turn Comparison Into Inspiration**
   If you find yourself admiring someone's accomplishments or lifestyle, see it as proof of what's possible rather than evidence of

what you're missing. Celebrate their achievements while recognizing that their success doesn't diminish your own potential.

2. **Curate Your Social Media Feed**

Social media is often a highlight reel. Be intentional about following accounts that inspire and uplift you, and unfollow or mute those that trigger comparison or self-doubt. You deserve a digital space that fuels positivity.

3. **Define Your Own Version of Success**

Spend time reflecting on what *you* want in life. What does success look like to you, on your own terms? Having clear, personal goals helps anchor you and reduces the urge to measure your life by someone else's milestones.

4. **Limit Your "Compare Zones"**

If there are specific situations or places where you feel extra pressure to compare, like social gatherings or scrolling late at night, set gentle boundaries. For example, limit your time on social media at night, or remind yourself of your strengths before stepping into a high-pressure environment.

5. **Focus on Personal Growth, Not Perfection**

Instead of striving to "be the best" or match someone else's life, set goals around your own growth. Ask yourself how you can become a better version of who you already are rather than chasing someone else's accomplishments.

Weekly Exercise: My Unique Path Journal

Each week, take some time to connect with your own journey. Here's how:

1. **Write Down Your Wins**

Each day or week, jot down a few personal achievements. These can be as big as completing a challenging project or as small as getting through a rough day with a positive outlook. These wins are proof of your unique journey and progress.

2. **Identify What Makes You, You**

   Make a list of your strengths, passions, and values. Think about the qualities you admire in yourself, the things you love to do, and the values that guide you. Keep this list somewhere visible and add to it over time.

3. **Visualize Your Own Path**

   Close your eyes and imagine where you want to go in life—not where anyone else is going, but what truly lights you up. What would a fulfilling life look like for you? This simple act of visualizing your own path can help you build a sense of confidence in your unique journey.

4. **Reflect at Week's End**

   Look back over your wins and strengths. Notice any growth, new realizations, or moments when you stayed true to yourself. This practice reinforces that you are on a valuable path, just as it is.

Final Thought

Comparison can make you feel like you're always running behind, but in reality, there's no race, and there's no one else you need to "beat." The people you admire or feel behind don't have your exact dreams, your unique potential, or your path—and that's what makes your journey so special. When you stop comparing and start celebrating your individuality, you give yourself permission to grow without pressure.

Remember, your journey is yours alone, and that's what gives it meaning. Trust that you're exactly where you need to be, and keep moving forward on your own terms. The more you focus on what you have to offer, the more you'll see that no comparison can measure up to the authenticity of being true to yourself.

CHAPTER 4

Rewriting Expectations

From a young age, we're surrounded by expectations—what we should achieve, how we should look, and who we should become. These expectations might come from family, society, or even the endless comparison encouraged by social media. It's easy to internalize these voices and mistake them for our own, carrying expectations that feel more like a burden than a dream. But whose life are we living if it's built on someone else's ideas?

Rewriting expectations means letting go of these "shoulds" and giving yourself permission to define your path. It's a process of asking, "What do *I* want? What actually feels right for *me*?" By challenging external expectations, you can finally rewrite a story that feels authentic and energizing, one where you are free to be exactly who you want to be.

How to Begin Rewriting Your Story

Letting go of external expectations doesn't mean disregarding everyone's advice or opinions, but rather learning to recognize what resonates with you versus what you've simply absorbed. Here are some steps to help you separate yourself from external pressures and start rewriting your own story:

1. **Identify Where Expectations Come From**

Write down some of the biggest "shoulds" you feel in your life, whether they're about career, relationships, appearance, or lifestyle. Next to each one, note where you think it came from—family, friends, society, or even an old version of yourself. Acknowledging the source helps you see that these ideas aren't always yours.

2. **Ask Yourself What You Truly Value**

Think about what genuinely matters to you. What do you want to be known for? What are the values that make you feel fulfilled? This reflection will guide you in making choices that feel right for *you* rather than choices made to meet someone else's expectations.

3. **Redefine Success on Your Terms**

Let go of one-size-fits-all definitions of success. What does success look like for you? Maybe it's not a high-powered career but a balanced life, a creative pursuit, or a strong sense of community. Your version of success is valid, no matter how unconventional it may seem.

4. **Challenge Your Inner Critic**

We often internalize external expectations as self-criticism. When you hear that voice telling you you're "not enough" or that you're "supposed to" be doing something else, pause and question it. Is this expectation true to who you are, or is it an old story you're ready to let go?

5. **Take Small Steps in Your New Direction**

Rewriting expectations is about action, too. Take a step toward the path that feels most true to you. Even small steps—like signing up for a class in something you love, or speaking up about what you actually want—are powerful in breaking the cycle of external expectations.

Weekly Exercise: The Expectation Release Journal

Each week, try this exercise to explore and release the expectations you've outgrown.

1. **Write Down a Limiting Expectation**
    Each week, choose one expectation that feels heavy or unaligned with who you are now. Maybe it's "I need to have a high-status job," or "I should always be agreeable." Write it down.

2. **Identify Its Source**
    Reflect on where this expectation came from. Was it a message you picked up from family, social media, or culture? Did it come from a friend's life or an old ambition that no longer suits you? By understanding the source, you start to see it more clearly as *someone else's* idea.

3. **Rewrite the Expectation**
    Transform the expectation into a statement that's authentic to you. If your expectation was "I need to have a high-status job," you might rewrite it as, "I want a career that makes me feel alive and purposeful." This is your chance to create a new, empowering message that fits *your* life.

4. **Reflect on How It Feels**
    Sit with the new statement. Notice how it feels to release the old expectation and embrace one that reflects your values. Writing about the relief or excitement you feel can reinforce this positive shift.

5. **Practice a New Step Each Week**
    Take one small action that aligns with your rewritten expectation. These actions will help you gain confidence in your path, one step at a time.

Final Thought

Letting go of expectations that aren't your own is like putting down a weight you didn't even realize you were carrying. The freedom that comes from honoring your own story—rather than someone else's—is a freedom that lets you live a life that feels like *yours*. You don't have to follow anyone else's script. You have permission to be exactly who you want to be and to create a path that feels meaningful.

Remember, you are allowed to change the narrative anytime you choose. Embracing your own vision for your life doesn't make you self-ish or rebellious—it makes you authentic. Let this be your story, your adventure, and the life that lights *you* up. You've always had the power to rewrite it.

CHAPTER 5

Who Are You Without the Filter?

We live in a world where almost everything has a filter—photos, opinions, and even personalities. It's normal to curate what we show to others, and sometimes even to ourselves, shaping how we're perceived and how we navigate the world. But beneath all the layers we project, there's a core self—someone who's real, unfiltered, and entirely unique. Understanding who you are at that core, without outside influence, can feel like an exploration of the most authentic, powerful parts of you.

Knowing your core self doesn't mean you're discarding everything you've picked up along the way. It means looking inward to find qualities and values that feel true, no matter who's around. Discovering who you are without the filter is a journey of recognizing what makes you tick, what brings you joy, and what aligns with your deepest values. This chapter is about removing the external layers and connecting to your most genuine self.

How to Discover Your Core Self

Finding who you are without the filter is about asking honest questions and exploring your natural preferences, not those shaped by what others expect. Here are some ways to start:

1. **Notice What Feels Most Natural**

   Pay attention to activities, people, and places where you feel at ease. When are you most comfortable being yourself? These moments often reveal parts of your core self that shine without needing any adjustments or filters.

2. **Identify Core Values**

   What are the values you hold that guide you, regardless of anyone else's opinion? Think about qualities that resonate deeply with you, like kindness, independence, or creativity. These values are anchors for your authentic self.

3. **Reflect on Childhood Interests**

   Often, our core self shows up in the things we loved before external expectations became louder—think back to what you loved as a child. What activities, dreams, or qualities did you enjoy most when you were young? There may be clues to your unfiltered passions there.

4. **Limit "Outside Voices"**

   Take a break from sources of influence, like social media, advice columns, or well-meaning friends. Spend some time reflecting in solitude or writing in a journal without external input. This quiet time can help you recognize your own thoughts and desires more clearly.

5. **Allow Space for Contradictions**

   We're all multifaceted, and discovering your core self doesn't mean sticking to one "type." Allow yourself to explore different parts of your personality, and don't worry if you have contrasting interests or traits. Embracing these contradictions often leads to a more genuine sense of self.

Weekly Exercise: The Authenticity Check-In

This week, try an authenticity check-in to uncover your core self in everyday life.

1. **Choose Three Words to Describe Yourself**

   Without overthinking, pick three words that resonate with you right now. Write them down, and reflect on why you chose each one. Are these traits that you embrace daily? Do they come from others' opinions, or do they feel like *your* words?

2. **Notice Your Reactions**

   Throughout the week, observe your reactions to various situations—whether it's a decision you make, a conversation, or even just a mood shift. Ask yourself, "Was this response truly me, or did it feel filtered?" These insights can help you recognize when you're being authentically yourself versus when you're adjusting for others.

3. **Reflect on Your Relationships**

   Think about the people in your life with whom you feel completely at ease. What about those relationships feels natural? These connections often mirror your core self, as you're likely being unfiltered and comfortable.

4. **Journal with the Prompt: "Who Am I Without Others Watching?"**

   Set aside 10-15 minutes to write freely, answering this question. Don't hold back, and don't worry about how it sounds. Imagine yourself in a space where no one is watching or judging, and let your true feelings emerge. Writing it out can help you see patterns that are most aligned with your core self.

5. **Practice One Unfiltered Moment Daily**

   Each day, try to express yourself without filtering or adjusting. It could be sharing an honest opinion, trying an activity just for you, or dressing in a way that feels authentic. Start small, and see how these moments feel as you build a habit of living unfiltered.

Final Thought

Understanding who you are without the filter isn't about becoming perfect or always knowing exactly who you are. It's about being open to your natural self and honoring that voice inside that says, "This is me." Each time you tune out external influences and listen to your own desires, preferences, and values, you're strengthening that core self.

Remember, your core self doesn't need to be polished or performative. It's the part of you that feels whole and complete, regardless of outside opinions or expectations. In a world that encourages so much "editing," embracing your unfiltered self is an act of courage and self-love. Trust that who you are, in the most genuine sense, is more than enough. Keep nurturing that authenticity, and watch how it opens up a life that feels true, fulfilling, and entirely yours.

CHAPTER 6

Recognizing Social Armor

In social situations, it's natural to adjust parts of ourselves depending on who we're with or where we are. This kind of adaptability can help us connect, make others feel comfortable, and sometimes, protect us from feeling vulnerable. But when we rely too heavily on these "masks" or layers of social armor, it can become harder to feel authentic. You might find yourself playing roles to fit in, hiding emotions, or adjusting your personality to meet the expectations of others.

Recognizing social armor means becoming aware of these masks and understanding when they're helpful and when they're holding you back. This chapter is about learning to spot when you're "putting on" a version of yourself and discovering ways to let those layers fall, so you can show up as the real you, with confidence and ease.

How to Identify and Drop Social Armor

Learning to recognize and release social armor can feel freeing, but it's a gradual process. Here are some ways to start identifying your masks and letting go:

1. **Notice When You're "Performing"**
    Pay attention to moments when you feel like you're adjusting your personality to meet a social expectation. Maybe you're pre-

tending to be more outgoing, or you're hiding your opinion to avoid conflict. These "performances" are often signs of social armor.

2.   **Recognize the Different Roles You Play**

Think about the roles you play in various parts of your life—like "the responsible one" with family, "the chill friend" in your friend group, or "the driven achiever" at work. Reflect on how much of each role feels true to who you are versus a role you take on to meet others' expectations.

3.   **Identify "Triggers" for Armor**

Certain situations may automatically make you reach for a mask, like meeting new people, being around authority figures, or engaging in group activities. Notice where and when these "triggers" come up, and ask yourself why. Understanding these moments can help you break the pattern.

4.   **Practice Vulnerability with Safe People**

Start by letting down your guard with people who make you feel comfortable and accepted. Practice sharing your true thoughts, showing your emotions, or admitting when you don't have it all figured out. These experiences will build your confidence in being unguarded.

5.   **Embrace Imperfections**

Social armor often comes from a desire to appear "perfect" or put together. Allowing yourself to be seen, flaws and all, can be empowering. Practice letting go of perfection, whether it's sharing a mistake you made, laughing at yourself, or admitting when you need help. The more you accept your imperfections, the less need you'll feel to wear a mask.

Weekly Exercise: The Armor Audit

This week, try an exercise to help you notice and gently remove the layers of social armor.

1.   **Take Inventory of Your Masks**
Start by writing down the different "masks" you think you wear. This could be a persona, like "the life of the party" or "the responsible friend." For each mask, ask yourself why you wear it and how it makes you feel. Do you feel more confident, or do you feel like you're hiding?

2.   **Reflect on a Recent Social Interaction**
Think back to a recent social interaction and ask yourself if you wore any masks. Why did you feel the need to adjust? How did it affect your energy or your mood? Reflecting on this will help you see when and why you reach for social armor.

3.   **Practice One Unfiltered Interaction**
Choose one interaction each day where you practice being your authentic self. This doesn't mean being vulnerable with everyone, but perhaps sharing a genuine thought, opinion, or emotion without filtering it. Notice how it feels to show up as you are, without the mask.

4.   **Journal Your Progress**
Each day, write a quick reflection on how you felt after dropping one piece of armor. Did you feel more comfortable? More exposed? More energized? Tracking these experiences will give you insight into what it's like to embrace authenticity.

5.   **Celebrate Small Wins**
Dropping social armor isn't easy, and it doesn't happen all at once. Each time you show up authentically, even in small ways, celebrate it as a win. These moments build the habit of being yourself and make it easier to let go of the masks over time.

Final Thought

Our social armor often feels like protection, but it can also keep us from fully connecting with ourselves and others. When you start to drop those masks, you may feel exposed at first, but you'll also start to feel lighter, more genuine, and more connected to the people who truly accept you. Your true self is more than enough, and the more you embrace that, the less you'll feel the need to hide.

Remember, you don't have to take off all your armor at once. Start with small steps, test the waters with people who support you, and trust that the real you is always worth showing. The journey of letting go of these masks isn't about becoming someone else—it's about finally letting yourself *be* the person you've always been.

CHAPTER 7

FOMO & Finding Real Fulfillment

In the age of constant updates and endless options, the fear of missing out—FOMO—has become almost impossible to escape. Scrolling through photos of friends at events, seeing people traveling, starting projects, or achieving something new can create a sense that we're missing out on something important. FOMO is often fueled by the idea that if we're not part of every opportunity, event, or trend, we're somehow "falling behind." But here's the reality: when we chase after everything, we lose the chance to focus on what actually brings us fulfillment.

Real fulfillment doesn't come from saying "yes" to everything. It comes from knowing what genuinely brings you joy, what aligns with your values, and what makes you feel grounded and whole. This chapter is about learning to handle FOMO by tuning in to what matters most to you and making choices that enrich your life from the inside out.

How to Deal with FOMO and Find Fulfillment

Here are a few ways to shift your mindset, minimize the grip of FOMO, and discover what brings you real, lasting joy:

1. **Define Your Priorities**
   Start by clarifying what genuinely matters to you. What are the

activities, values, and goals that bring you a sense of purpose and happiness? When you know what matters most, it becomes easier to turn down distractions that don't align with those priorities.

2. **Practice "Selective Yes"**

Instead of saying "yes" out of fear of missing out, practice "selective yes" by only agreeing to opportunities or events that resonate with you. Ask yourself, "Will this make me happy or help me grow?" If not, it's okay to say no. Protecting your time for meaningful experiences is one of the most powerful ways to reduce FOMO.

3. **Limit Social Media Consumption**

Social media can make FOMO worse by creating a highlight reel of everyone else's best moments. Try limiting your time online or setting specific times to check social media. Taking a step back allows you to focus on your own life and reduces the pressure to "keep up" with everyone else.

4. **Reflect on Your "Why"**

If you feel FOMO creeping in, pause and ask yourself why you want to be part of a certain experience. Is it out of genuine interest, or are you driven by a fear of being left out? This simple reflection can help you make decisions that are based on your own needs, not external pressure.

5. **Invest in Fulfilling Activities**

Make time for the things that truly fill you up—whether it's reading, working on a creative project, spending time with loved ones, or exploring a hobby. These activities bring a different kind of joy, one that's not dependent on outside approval or trends.

Weekly Exercise: The Fulfillment Journal

To help you tune into what brings real fulfillment, try this weekly exercise:

1. **List What Made You Feel Fulfilled This Week**

    At the end of each day or week, jot down a few moments that genuinely brought you joy. Maybe it was a meaningful conversation, completing a creative project, or simply spending a relaxing evening on your own. Focusing on these moments helps you recognize what fills you up.

2. **Reflect on FOMO Moments**

    When you notice feelings of FOMO, write them down and reflect on what triggered them. Was it social media, a conversation, or an event invite? Think about whether participating in that experience would align with your values or just be a distraction.

3. **Create a "Fulfillment Filter"**

    Based on your reflections, create a personal "fulfillment filter"—a set of questions that guide your decisions. Questions like, "Does this support my growth?" or "Will this bring me real joy?" can help you make intentional choices rather than reactive ones.

4. **Set Fulfillment Goals for the Week**

    Choose one or two activities or goals that bring genuine satisfaction, like working on a passion project, spending time with loved ones, or learning something new. By setting these goals, you create a week that's more aligned with what truly matters to you.

5. **Celebrate the Power of No**

    If you turned down an opportunity because it didn't align with your fulfillment filter, celebrate that choice! Recognizing the power of saying "no" reminds you that you're in control of your life and that real joy doesn't require constant involvement in everything.

Final Thought

FOMO can make us feel like life is happening elsewhere, that everyone else has something we're missing. But fulfillment isn't about filling every gap—it's about finding the specific things that make your life meaningful. When you tune in to what genuinely brings you joy, you'll notice that FOMO loses its power over you, replaced by a deep sense of satisfaction in the life you're creating.

Remember, your life doesn't need to be a highlight reel. Real fulfillment comes from experiences and choices that resonate with you and your values. Trust that what's meant for you will align with your path. When you make choices from this place of alignment, you're no longer just "keeping up"; you're creating a life that's all your own. Choose moments that truly matter to you, and watch how fulfillment begins to take the place of FOMO.

CHAPTER 8

Detox: Small Shifts for Big Impact

Technology connects us in powerful ways, but constant screen time can also leave us feeling mentally cluttered, anxious, or even detached from real-life experiences. When every moment is accompanied by a notification or screen, it becomes harder to fully appreciate the world around us. Taking a break from screens—even for a short period—can help you reconnect with yourself, reduce stress, and make space for what truly matters.

A digital detox doesn't have to mean unplugging completely or for long stretches. Even small shifts, like setting aside "no-screen" times or reclaiming a few minutes of tech-free solitude, can create a positive impact on your mood, focus, and well-being. This chapter explores simple, manageable steps to start your own digital detox and experience the benefits of a more balanced relationship with technology.

Small Shifts to Start Your Digital Detox

You don't have to overhaul your entire life to create space from screens. Here are a few practical, low-pressure ways to begin incorporating digital detox practices into your routine:

1. **Designate "No-Phone" Zones**

   Create specific areas or times where screens are off-limits, like your bedroom, at meals, or during your morning and evening routines. By giving yourself these screen-free zones, you create pockets of calm and improve your focus on the present moment.

2. **Set Screen-Free Hours**

   Choose a certain time of day when you intentionally go without screens, like the first hour after waking up or the last hour before bed. Use this time for something meaningful or relaxing, like journaling, stretching, or enjoying a cup of coffee with no distractions.

3. **Practice the "One-Hour Check-In"**

   When you do check your phone or log on, set a timer to remind yourself to take a break after an hour. Use these breaks to stretch, take a few deep breaths, or look out the window. Regular check-ins can help you become more conscious of your screen time.

4. **Turn Off Non-Essential Notifications**

   Each ping and vibration pulls your attention back to the screen. By disabling notifications for non-essential apps, you regain control over when and how often you check your phone. You can always check these apps later, on your own time.

5. **Use the 20-20-20 Rule**

   For every 20 minutes of screen time, take a 20-second break to look at something 20 feet away. This not only helps reduce eye strain but also brings your awareness back to the present, offering a mini digital detox throughout the day.

Weekly Exercise: The One-Day Digital Detox

This week, set aside one day (or even a half-day) for a deeper digital detox. Here's a simple guide to help you plan a screen-free day that leaves you feeling refreshed:

1. **Choose Your Detox Day**

    Pick a day that feels manageable—perhaps a weekend or a day when you don't have pressing digital obligations. Let friends or family know that you'll be offline to avoid any surprise messages or calls.

2. **Plan a Few Screen-Free Activities**

    To avoid the temptation to reach for your phone, make a list of activities you'd enjoy without screens, like reading a physical book, going for a walk, cooking, or doing a creative project. These activities can keep you occupied while also being restorative.

3. **Create a "Phone Home"**

    Designate a specific place to keep your phone for the day. Putting it somewhere out of reach can help reduce the temptation to check it. Consider putting it in another room or setting it to "Do Not Disturb" mode.

4. **Notice the Moments of Urge**

    Throughout the day, you might feel the impulse to check your phone or other screens. When this happens, take a breath and ask yourself what's triggering the urge. Sometimes it's boredom, other times it's habit. Identifying these triggers helps you understand your digital habits and find alternatives.

5. **End with Reflection**

    At the end of your digital detox day, take a few minutes to journal or reflect on the experience. How did you feel without screens? Did you notice any positive shifts, like a calmer mind or a greater sense of presence? This reflection can help you appreciate the value of taking a break from technology.

Final Thought

Taking breaks from screens isn't about rejecting technology—it's about creating balance so that you can experience life fully, both online and offline. The small shifts you make in your daily routine can bring a greater sense of calm, focus, and real connection to the people and places around you. These moments without screens help you be more present in your own life, letting you appreciate the quiet moments and small details that might otherwise go unnoticed.

Remember, you don't have to disconnect entirely to reap the benefits of a digital detox. By carving out these screen-free moments, you're giving yourself permission to recharge, to breathe, and to reconnect with the world right in front of you. Every small shift you make creates a ripple, bringing more balance and mindfulness to your life, one moment at a time.

CHAPTER 9

The Power of Silence

In a world filled with constant noise—social media, notifications, music, and the hum of everyday life—true silence can feel rare and almost uncomfortable. We're so used to filling every quiet moment that silence itself might even seem awkward or unsettling. But silence is a powerful space for growth, reflection, and self-discovery. It's in those quiet moments that we can hear our own thoughts clearly, connect with our true emotions, and begin to understand what we genuinely want and need.

Embracing silence isn't about isolating yourself or rejecting the world around you. It's about creating space to let your own voice be heard. Silence allows for introspection, clarity, and grounding, helping you tune into the parts of yourself that are often drowned out by daily noise. This chapter is about learning to appreciate silence, finding peace in it, and using it as a tool to connect with your inner self.

How to Start Embracing Silence

Silence can feel intimidating at first, but with time, you may come to find it comforting and enriching. Here are a few ways to start incorporating intentional silence into your life:

1. **Start Your Day with Quiet Time**

Begin each morning with a few minutes of silence before checking your phone or engaging with others. Sit quietly with your thoughts, or enjoy a slow cup of tea or coffee without distractions. This gentle start can help you set a calm tone for the day and allow space for your own thoughts to emerge.

2. **Take Mini Silence Breaks**

Throughout your day, take small breaks where you sit quietly, even if it's just for five minutes. These moments can be as simple as sitting in your room, taking a walk, or closing your eyes in a quiet space. Regular breaks from noise help you stay centered and aware of your inner state.

3. **Practice Mindful Listening**

When silence feels uncomfortable, try focusing on any faint sounds around you, like birds chirping, the wind, or even your own breath. This simple practice can make silence feel more grounding and alive, helping you ease into the stillness without feeling overwhelmed.

4. **Journal in Silence**

Writing can be a wonderful companion to silence. Set aside 10-15 minutes each day to journal in complete quiet, allowing your thoughts to flow without outside influence. Let this space be a time for reflection on what's happening in your life and how you feel in the moment.

5. **End Your Day with Silent Reflection**

Before going to bed, spend a few minutes sitting quietly and reflecting on your day. Avoid screens, talking, or distractions. This evening silence helps you process the day's events, calm your mind, and transition peacefully into rest.

Weekly Exercise: The Power of Silence Meditation

To deepen your comfort with silence, try this weekly meditation exercise. It's a way to spend time in quiet contemplation and practice being fully present with yourself.

1. **Find a Comfortable Space**

    Choose a place where you won't be interrupted. It could be a quiet corner of your room, a park bench, or any place where you feel relaxed and safe.

2. **Set a Timer for 10-15 Minutes**

    Start with a short period, like 10 minutes, and gradually increase the time as you grow more comfortable with silence. Set your phone on silent and keep it out of reach to avoid distractions.

3. **Sit Quietly and Focus on Your Breath**

    Take a few deep breaths to settle in, and then let your breath flow naturally. Focus on the sensation of each inhale and exhale, allowing your mind to quiet. If thoughts arise, simply notice them without judgment and let them pass.

4. **Observe What Comes Up**

    In the silence, you may notice emotions, memories, or ideas rising to the surface. Acknowledge them, but try not to dwell. The goal is not to solve problems or analyze, but to be a neutral observer of your inner world.

5. **Reflect and Journal**

    After your silence meditation, take a few minutes to journal about your experience. What thoughts or emotions surfaced? How did it feel to sit in silence? These reflections can provide insight into what's happening within and help you become more at ease with quiet moments.

Final Thought

Silence is a gift that brings clarity, calm, and self-awareness. In a noisy world, the choice to embrace quiet moments can feel like a small act of rebellion, a way to honor your inner life and your personal growth. Silence isn't about absence—it's about presence, allowing you to be fully with yourself, undistracted and open to whatever might arise.

Remember, silence is a practice, one that grows easier and more natural with time. The more you embrace it, the more you'll discover the hidden wisdom and strength that come from simply being with yourself. In the quiet, you'll find clarity and connection, and you may realize that some of the answers you've been searching for were already within you, waiting to be heard.

So let silence be a place of comfort, a pause from the noise, and a pathway to a deeper understanding of who you are. Embrace these moments, and let them lead you closer to the person you're becoming.

CHAPTER 10

Setting Boundaries with the World

Boundaries are the invisible lines that protect your energy, time, and emotional well-being. They're not walls to shut others out but gentle perimeters that help you define where your comfort zone ends and where outside demands begin. Setting boundaries is an act of self-respect; it allows you to maintain your authenticity, even when the world around you may pull you in different directions.

Boundaries can be challenging to set, especially if you worry about disappointing others or fear being misunderstood. But healthy boundaries are essential for protecting your mental and emotional energy. They give you the freedom to focus on what feels true to you, rather than being constantly swayed by the expectations, needs, or moods of others. This chapter is about learning how to build and communicate boundaries that support your growth, honor your values, and preserve your authenticity.

How to Build Boundaries That Support Your Well-Being

Setting boundaries can feel daunting, but these steps can help you create boundaries that feel respectful, empowering, and manageable.

1.   **Identify Your Needs and Limits**
The first step in setting boundaries is knowing where they're needed. Reflect on situations that often leave you feeling drained, uncomfortable, or resentful. Are there specific people, places, or types of interactions that cross your comfort zone? Knowing your limits helps you define boundaries that will support your well-being.

2.   **Clarify Your Values**
Boundaries become easier to set when they align with your core values. What's most important to you—authenticity, growth, peace, time for creativity? When your boundaries protect what matters to you, they feel purposeful and worth holding, even when it's difficult.

3.   **Start Small and Be Specific**
Begin with small, manageable boundaries. For example, if you need uninterrupted time to work, try setting a "do not disturb" period for an hour. If you feel overwhelmed by frequent texts or calls, let people know you'll respond during certain times. Specific, small steps make boundary-setting feel achievable and realistic.

4.   **Communicate with Kindness and Clarity**
Expressing boundaries can feel intimidating, especially if you're concerned about how others will react. Approach boundary-setting as a conversation, not a demand. Be clear and honest, using "I" statements, like "I need some quiet time in the morning to feel focused," or "I'd appreciate if we could schedule calls ahead of time." Clear, kind communication minimizes confusion and builds mutual respect.

5.   **Practice Saying "No" Without Guilt**
Saying "no" can be tough, but it's a powerful way to uphold your boundaries. Remember, a thoughtful "no" respects both your needs and the other person's right to clarity. If guilt arises, remind

yourself that honoring your needs is not selfish—it's essential for building healthy relationships and a balanced life.

6.   **Hold Your Boundaries Consistently**
People may test or forget your boundaries, so gentle reminders might be necessary. Holding your boundaries consistently, even in small ways, reinforces them over time. Each time you honor your boundaries, you're building confidence in your ability to protect your energy and live authentically.

Weekly Exercise: The Boundary Blueprint

This week, create a "boundary blueprint" to help you identify and establish boundaries in a way that feels true to you.

1.   **List Your Non-Negotiables**
Make a list of your "non-negotiables"—the values, needs, and limits you want to protect. Examples might include quiet time in the morning, the right to express your opinions, or uninterrupted study or creative time. These are the anchors for your boundaries.

2.   **Identify Your Biggest "Energy Drains"**
Think about what situations or interactions tend to leave you feeling depleted. These might include unplanned commitments, toxic conversations, or expectations that don't align with your goals. Understanding what drains you helps you create boundaries that safeguard your energy.

3.   **Craft Three Specific Boundaries**
Choose three small but meaningful boundaries to focus on this week. They might be things like setting specific times to check your phone, spending time alone daily, or limiting social events to a manageable number. Write these boundaries down and reflect on why they're important.

4.   **Track Your Progress**
Throughout the week, note how you feel when you uphold these

boundaries. Did you feel more energized, calm, or authentic? Reflecting on your experiences helps reinforce the positive impact of boundaries, motivating you to continue setting them.

5. **Adjust as Needed**

Boundaries are flexible and can be adjusted as you grow and your needs change. If you notice certain boundaries aren't working or need refinement, don't be afraid to revisit and adjust them. Boundaries that evolve with you remain effective and aligned with your well-being.

Final Thought

Setting boundaries may feel uncomfortable at first, but each step you take builds your confidence in honoring what matters to you. Boundaries aren't about rejecting others; they're about creating a life where you can show up fully and authentically. Each time you hold a boundary, you're affirming that your energy, time, and peace are worth protecting.

Remember, boundaries are not barriers—they're bridges to a healthier, more balanced life where you can express yourself freely and connect with others without sacrificing your well-being. Embrace this journey of boundary-setting as a gift to yourself, and know that you deserve the peace, respect, and authenticity that boundaries bring. Let this practice be a reminder that you are worthy of living life on your terms, protecting your energy, and being true to who you are.

Rediscovering the Real You

CHAPTER 11

What is Self-Awareness?

Self-awareness is the practice of truly seeing yourself—not just your achievements, job title, or the roles you play in others' lives, but the core of who you are. It's about recognizing your values, your strengths, your challenges, and your motivations. Self-awareness isn't measured by external success but by your ability to understand, accept, and grow from the unique qualities that make you *you*.

In a world that often equates worth with productivity, status, or recognition, self-awareness can help you tap into a deeper understanding of yourself beyond the labels. It gives you the power to feel grounded in your identity, even when life is unpredictable. Self-awareness also helps you live more authentically by acting in ways that are true to you, rather than seeking constant validation or approval. This chapter is about building that inner clarity and learning to see yourself with acceptance and honesty.

Steps to Build Self-Awareness

Here are some gentle, practical steps to help you understand and connect with who you are beyond external achievements:

1. **Reflect on Your Values**
    Values are the qualities or principles that matter most to you, like

honesty, compassion, or creativity. Ask yourself, "What principles do I want to live by?" and "What makes me feel fulfilled and at peace?" Reflecting on your values will help you understand what truly drives you, beyond external pressures.

2. **Identify Your Strengths and Growth Areas**

Knowing your strengths builds confidence, while recognizing growth areas keeps you grounded and open to improvement. Take some time to write down your strengths, the things that come naturally to you, as well as areas you'd like to develop. This balanced view helps you see yourself honestly without judgment.

3. **Understand Your Emotional Patterns**

Emotions offer insight into who you are. Notice which situations make you feel energized, which ones drain you, and where you feel most yourself. Tracking emotional patterns can help you understand what aligns with your true self and what may be leading you away from it.

4. **Practice Self-Compassion**

Self-awareness requires a foundation of self-compassion. As you reflect on your experiences and traits, practice acceptance rather than judgment. Self-compassion is key to truly understanding and appreciating yourself, even when you see areas for growth.

5. **Challenge Labels and Expectations**

We all carry labels, some from others and some self-imposed. Question any labels that don't feel authentic, like "the overachiever" or "the people-pleaser." Consider who you are beyond these labels, and ask yourself, "What do I want to be defined by?" Releasing limiting labels helps you explore who you are without unnecessary pressure.

Weekly Exercise: The Self-Awareness Journal

This week, try keeping a self-awareness journal to gain deeper insights into who you are beyond achievements or external labels.

1. **Identify Core Values and Write About Them**

   Begin by listing five to seven core values that resonate with you. Write a few sentences about each, explaining why it's meaningful and how it shapes your life. Returning to these values reminds you of the inner compass that guides your choices and actions.

2. **Describe Three "True to You" Moments**

   Think back to moments in your life when you felt completely yourself, perhaps with certain people, places, or activities. Describe these moments in detail. Noticing where you feel free to be yourself helps you understand the qualities that define your authentic self.

3. **Reflect on Recent Emotions**

   At the end of each day, write down a few emotions you felt and what triggered them. Were they related to your values, strengths, or boundaries? Were they responses to outside pressures? This practice helps you recognize which situations support your true self and which may lead you away from it.

4. **List What You'd Like to Understand Better About Yourself**

   Self-awareness is a journey, not a destination. Make a list of any traits, habits, or experiences you'd like to explore further. Maybe you're curious about why certain things make you anxious or what drives your sense of accomplishment. These are areas you can reflect on over time.

5. **Celebrate Small Wins of Self-Discovery**

   Each day, note a small win that brought you closer to understanding yourself. It could be noticing a pattern in your emotions or realizing how a specific activity aligns with your values. These small steps reinforce your journey of self-awareness and remind you of the power of knowing yourself.

Final Thought

Self-awareness is an ongoing journey. The more you understand who you are, the less you feel defined by titles, achievements, or other people's expectations. By looking inward, you're building a strong foundation rooted in acceptance and clarity. This foundation gives you confidence in the choices you make, because they come from a place of true alignment, not external pressure.

Remember, self-awareness isn't about perfection or having everything figured out; it's about curiosity, compassion, and growth. Embrace this process, knowing that each small step you take leads to a deeper connection with your true self. The power of self-awareness is the freedom it brings—freedom to live authentically, make choices aligned with your values, and create a life that reflects who you really are.

CHAPTER 12

The Search for Aliveness

In the midst of everyday routines, responsibilities, and expectations, it's easy to lose touch with the things that truly light us up. We often get so focused on productivity and goals that we can forget to pause and ask ourselves, "What makes me feel *alive?*" Aliveness is more than just being busy or checking things off a list; it's about experiencing a sense of energy, joy, and purpose. It's the feeling that reminds you of who you are at your core, of what makes life vibrant and meaningful.

This chapter is about rediscovering those sources of joy and connection, the experiences and interests that bring out your passion, playfulness, and sense of wonder. When you know what makes you feel alive, you gain a guidepost for a life that's fulfilling and uniquely yours. Reconnecting with your personal sources of joy isn't just self-care; it's self-discovery. It's about finding out what fills you with energy and excitement, so you can bring more of those moments into your life.

How to Find and Reconnect with What Brings You Joy

If you're not sure what makes you feel alive, don't worry—sometimes it takes time to rediscover or explore new interests. Here are some steps to help you connect with what brings you joy:

1. **Reflect on Your Passions and Interests**
Think about activities, people, or places that energize you. Do you feel alive when you're outdoors, immersed in art, learning something new, or helping others? Reflect on what you're naturally drawn to, even if it's been a while since you engaged with it.

2. **Revisit Childhood Joys**
Our childhood often holds clues about what brings us joy—interests we pursued for pure enjoyment without worrying about productivity. Think back to activities you loved as a kid. Did you enjoy being creative, playing sports, reading, or exploring nature? Reconnecting with these interests can reignite old sparks of joy.

3. **Notice When You Feel Present and Engaged**
Pay attention to moments when you feel fully absorbed, where time seems to fly by and you feel completely present. These moments of flow often indicate an activity that brings a sense of aliveness. Whether it's a hobby, a conversation, or a new experience, note when you feel engaged and energized.

4. **Explore New Experiences**
Sometimes, discovering what makes you feel alive involves stepping out of your comfort zone. Try something you've been curious about, even if it's unfamiliar. Join a class, volunteer, try a new sport, or travel somewhere you've never been. These new experiences can open doors to unexpected joys.

5. **Let Go of Perfectionism**
The pursuit of joy isn't about doing things perfectly or impressing others; it's about allowing yourself to experience life fully. Let go of the need to be "good" at what you try. Allow yourself to play, explore, and enjoy without pressure, knowing that aliveness comes from the experience itself, not the outcome.

Weekly Exercise: The Joy Inventory

This week, try a "Joy Inventory" to help you reconnect with what makes you feel alive. The goal is to discover, deepen, and celebrate the sources of joy that bring meaning and energy into your life.

1. **Make a Joy List**
    Write down a list of activities, people, places, or memories that bring you happiness, energy, or calm. Don't filter or over-think—list anything that makes you smile or feel uplifted, from simple pleasures like reading to big passions like travel or art.

2. **Choose One Joyful Activity**
    Pick one item from your list to incorporate into your week, even if only for a few minutes each day. Maybe it's painting, hiking, dancing, or reconnecting with an old friend. Give yourself permission to prioritize this joyful activity and enjoy it without distraction.

3. **Reflect on How You Feel**
    After each joyful activity, write down how you felt before, during, and after. Did you feel more relaxed, energized, or inspired? Recognizing the impact of these activities on your well-being reinforces the value of making time for them.

4. **Plan a New Joyful Experience**
    Think of something you've always wanted to try, but haven't made time for. It could be a creative project, a weekend road trip, or learning a new skill. Schedule a time to try this experience, and approach it with curiosity and openness, not worrying about the outcome.

5. **Celebrate Small Moments of Joy**
    Joy isn't always about big events. Make it a habit to notice and appreciate small moments that bring you joy each day—a sunny morning, a good meal, a favorite song, or a conversation with

someone who lifts you up. Write these moments down in a journal to remind yourself of the everyday sources of joy.

Final Thought

Life can be busy and full of obligations, but when we reconnect with what brings us joy, we bring color and energy back into our everyday routines. Finding what makes you feel alive isn't about escaping reality; it's about enriching it with moments that make you feel more like yourself. When you know what lights you up, you have a compass that guides you toward a life that's meaningful, fulfilling, and full of vitality.

Remember, joy doesn't have to be grand or impressive. It's often found in the simplest experiences, the things that make you feel present, connected, and at ease. So make time to explore, play, and celebrate what makes you feel truly alive. Embrace these moments of joy, and let them become stepping stones toward a life where you're not just living but *thriving*. The more you prioritize what brings you joy, the more you'll find yourself on a path that feels authentic and deeply fulfilling.

CHAPTER 13

Authenticity: Being vs. Becoming

Authenticity is one of the most valued qualities we strive for—being true to ourselves in every situation. But as we grow and evolve, we're constantly balancing two sides of ourselves: the "being," who we are at our core, and the "becoming," the person we're growing into. Navigating between these two can sometimes be tricky. Are we pursuing genuine growth that feels aligned with who we truly are, or are we forcing change to meet expectations, trends, or external pressures?

This chapter is about understanding the difference between authentic growth and forced change. Growth that feels real will always connect back to your core values, while forced change often feels uncomfortable or hollow. Embracing this balance of "being" and "becoming" allows you to honor your unique journey, letting your growth unfold naturally rather than trying to mold yourself into something you're not.

How to Navigate Between Being and Becoming

Finding the balance between staying true to yourself and evolving takes mindfulness and self-reflection. Here are ways to help you distinguish between genuine growth and forced change:

1. **Reflect on Your Core Self**

    Take time to reconnect with who you are at your core—your values, passions, and natural qualities. Ask yourself, "Who am I when I'm at my most authentic?" Understanding the traits that make you, *you*, is key to recognizing when a change is truly aligned with your core self.

2. **Set Intentions for Growth**

    Growth is powerful when it's rooted in intentionality. Consider why you're pursuing a specific goal or change. Is it something you genuinely want, or are you influenced by trends, societal pressure, or the expectations of others? Intentional growth feels purposeful and fulfilling because it aligns with your personal values and long-term vision.

3. **Embrace Self-Acceptance While Evolving**

    Authenticity means accepting yourself as you are, even as you work on becoming who you want to be. Growth shouldn't come from a place of self-rejection or pressure to "fix" yourself, but from a genuine desire to expand your strengths and explore your potential. This approach makes growth feel natural, not forced.

4. **Differentiate Between Inspiration and Imitation**

    It's easy to be inspired by others' lives, especially with constant exposure to social media. But there's a difference between drawing inspiration and feeling the need to imitate someone else's path. Ask yourself, "Does this feel like *my* journey, or am I trying to fit someone else's mold?" Authentic growth follows your unique trajectory.

5. **Notice Signs of Forced Change**

    Forced change often feels heavy, uncomfortable, or inauthentic. If you're constantly second-guessing yourself, feeling drained, or struggling to stay motivated, it could be a sign that the change you're pursuing doesn't align with your true self. Trust these signals and don't be afraid to pivot toward growth that feels more genuine.

Weekly Exercise: The Authentic Growth Check-In

This week, take some time to explore whether your current goals and growth reflect genuine alignment or if they feel forced. This exercise will help you clarify the difference and bring more authenticity into your journey.

1. **List Your Current Goals**

    Begin by listing your current goals or areas where you're working on self-improvement. Be honest with yourself—whether they're personal, academic, social, or career-related, write down what you're currently striving toward.

2. **Reflect on Why Each Goal Matters**

    For each goal, write a few sentences about why it's important to you. Are you pursuing it because it genuinely excites you, or is it based on external pressure or a desire to please others? Reflecting on the *why* will help you see which goals feel aligned and which may be driven by outside influences.

3. **Identify Where You Feel Most Authentic**

    Think about moments when you've felt completely yourself. What activities, settings, or relationships bring out your most authentic qualities? Jot down a few words or descriptions of these moments. They'll serve as reminders of your core self as you pursue growth.

4. **Check for Authentic Alignment**

    Compare your list of goals to the qualities or experiences that make you feel most authentic. Do your goals align with who you naturally are, or do they seem at odds with your core self? If any goals feel forced, consider ways you might adjust them to better align with your true self.

5. **Set One Authentic Goal for the Week**

    Choose one goal or activity that feels genuinely exciting or meaningful to you and commit to it for the week. This could be something as simple as practicing a hobby you love, reconnecting with friends, or focusing on personal growth that feels natural. Notice how pursuing an authentic goal affects your energy and mindset.

Final Thought

The journey between "being" and "becoming" is not about reaching some fixed version of yourself. It's about honoring who you are while embracing the natural changes and growth that come with experience. When you allow growth to flow from a place of authenticity, you'll feel more grounded and empowered on your path.

Remember, authentic growth isn't about becoming someone different; it's about becoming *more* of who you already are. When you're true to yourself, every step of your journey will feel like it belongs to you, regardless of how fast or slow it seems compared to others. Trust in your unique path, honoring both who you are and who you're becoming, and you'll find a balance that feels right for you. In a world full of pressure to constantly change, your authentic growth will be a reflection of the person you truly are—beautiful, evolving, and entirely enough.

CHAPTER 14

Embracing Emotions Without Shame

Emotions are powerful signals, each carrying messages about what we need, value, and experience in our lives. But in a world that often celebrates positivity and "good vibes only," we can start to view certain emotions—like sadness, anger, or anxiety—as "bad" or something to be avoided. Over time, this can lead to a habit of suppressing or ignoring our feelings, and even feeling shame for experiencing them. Yet, every emotion, whether comfortable or challenging, is valid and meaningful. Each feeling provides insight into our inner world and can be a guide on our journey toward growth and self-understanding.

Embracing all of your emotions means learning to accept them as part of your human experience without judging or silencing them. This chapter is about removing the labels of "good" and "bad" from emotions, so you can start listening to and learning from what they're trying to tell you. By welcoming your full emotional range, you build a deeper connection with yourself, one that is rooted in acceptance and compassion rather than shame.

How to Embrace Emotions Without Shame

Learning to accept your emotions as they come is a practice that takes patience and self-compassion. Here are some steps to help you embrace your emotions and find meaning in all that you feel:

1. **Acknowledge Your Feelings as They Are**
   The first step to embracing your emotions is to acknowledge them without trying to change or judge them. When a strong feeling arises, take a moment to say to yourself, "This is what I'm feeling right now." Giving a name to your emotions helps validate your experience and makes it easier to process.

2. **Remove Labels of "Good" and "Bad"**
   Practice viewing your emotions as information, not as something that needs to be controlled or categorized as "positive" or "negative." Whether it's joy, anger, sadness, or excitement, all emotions are simply signals trying to guide you. By removing judgment, you create space to understand what each feeling is communicating.

3. **Explore the Message Behind Each Emotion**
   Each emotion often carries a deeper message. Ask yourself, "What might this feeling be trying to tell me?" For example, sadness might indicate a need for comfort, anger might highlight a boundary being crossed, and joy may signal alignment with your values. Emotions are your mind and body's way of guiding you toward what you need.

4. **Practice Self-Compassion During Difficult Emotions**
   Challenging emotions can trigger self-criticism or shame, especially if you've been taught that these feelings are "wrong" or "weak." Practice self-compassion by reminding yourself that everyone experiences a full range of emotions and that it's okay to feel exactly as you do. You're allowed to feel what you feel, and there's no need to apologize for it.

5.   **Express Your Feelings in Healthy Ways**

Embracing your emotions doesn't mean letting them control you—it means honoring and expressing them constructively. You might write in a journal, talk to a friend, create art, or go for a walk. Finding healthy outlets helps you process emotions and allows them to flow through you rather than becoming stuck or overwhelming.

Weekly Exercise: The Emotion Acceptance Journal

This week, try keeping an "Emotion Acceptance Journal" to help you embrace your feelings without judgment. This exercise is designed to help you tune into your emotions, understand their messages, and practice accepting them as they are.

1.   **Check In with Yourself Daily**

Each day, set aside a few minutes to check in with your emotions. Write down the primary feelings you experienced and any situations that may have triggered them. This simple check-in helps you stay connected to your inner world and allows you to observe your emotions without reacting to them immediately.

2.   **Name and Accept Each Emotion**

For each emotion you record, write a short sentence acknowledging it. For example, "I feel sad because I miss my friend," or "I feel anxious about an upcoming deadline." By naming your feelings, you validate them, and by accepting them, you release the need to fight or change them.

3.   **Reflect on the Message**

Choose one emotion each day and take a few minutes to explore what it might be trying to communicate. What need or value is this emotion highlighting? Reflecting on the message helps you see each emotion as meaningful rather than something to hide or dismiss.

4. **Practice Self-Compassion Statements**

If you feel judgment creeping in, try a self-compassion statement, such as, "It's okay to feel this way," or "This feeling is part of being human." Practicing self-compassion reminds you that emotions aren't flaws—they're part of your journey, and you deserve understanding, not shame.

5. **End with Gratitude for Your Emotions**

At the end of each entry, write down one thing you're grateful for about your emotions. It could be gratitude for the way they guide you, for the depth they bring to your life, or for the lessons they help you learn. This practice shifts your perspective, helping you see emotions as a gift rather than a burden.

Final Thought

Embracing all your emotions without shame is a powerful act of self-love. When you allow yourself to feel fully, you build a deeper understanding of who you are and what you need. Emotions aren't meant to be controlled or dismissed; they're meant to be listened to, honored, and felt. By welcoming your full emotional range, you strengthen your connection to yourself and move closer to living an authentic life.

Remember, each emotion is a teacher, and each feeling has value. Trust that your emotions are valid and worthy of acknowledgment. With practice, you'll find that embracing your emotions, rather than avoiding or hiding them, brings a sense of peace and self-acceptance. Let this practice remind you that you're whole just as you are—feeling deeply, expressing honestly, and living fully. Embrace each emotion as a meaningful part of your journey, and let them lead you toward a deeper, more compassionate understanding of yourself.

CHAPTER 15

Why Your Voice Matters

In a world where opinions, advice, and feedback are shared constantly—online, in social circles, and even in our own minds—it's easy to feel lost in the noise. We're often bombarded with voices telling us who we should be, what we should care about, and how we should live. But at the core of each of us, there is a unique voice—a perspective, a way of seeing the world, and a set of values that are all our own

Finding and trusting your own voice means rediscovering who you are beyond outside influences and pressures. It's about speaking up for what matters to you, making choices that align with your inner truth, and having the confidence to express your thoughts and feelings, even when they might go against the grain. This chapter is about reconnecting with that inner voice, so you can stand strong in your own truth and navigate the world without losing sight of who you are.

Steps to Find and Trust Your Own Voice

Reclaiming your voice isn't about shutting out others—it's about making space for yourself and listening to what's true for you. Here are some ways to help you find and trust your own voice in a world full of external noise:

1. **Spend Time in Reflection**

   Taking time to reflect is essential for reconnecting with your voice. Journaling, meditating, or simply spending time alone with your thoughts allows you to listen to yourself without interruption. Ask yourself, "What do I truly believe?" and "What do I genuinely care about?" Let these reflections guide you.

2. **Identify Your Values**

   Your values act as a compass, guiding your voice. Think about what matters most to you—honesty, kindness, growth, creativity, or justice. When you know your core values, you can let them shape your words and decisions, making it easier to speak up and act in ways that feel aligned with your true self.

3. **Question Outside Influences**

   Notice when outside influences, such as social media, friends, or family, start to sway your thoughts and actions. When you feel pressured to adopt certain opinions or choices, ask yourself, "Is this my truth, or is it someone else's?" Practicing this distinction strengthens your ability to trust your own beliefs.

4. **Speak Up in Small Ways**

   Reclaiming your voice doesn't mean making bold statements right away. Start by expressing your thoughts and feelings in smaller, everyday moments. Whether it's sharing an opinion in a group conversation or stating a preference with friends, these small steps help you build confidence in your voice.

5. **Practice Self-Validation**

   Learn to validate your thoughts and feelings internally, rather than seeking approval from others. Trust that your perspective is valuable, even if it's not validated externally. Remind yourself that your voice matters simply because it's yours, and you don't need others to agree for it to be true.

Weekly Exercise: The Voice Journal

This week, try keeping a "Voice Journal" to help you explore and strengthen your own voice. This exercise is designed to guide you through a series of reflections and actions that will bring you closer to your authentic self-expression.

1. **Identify Your Core Beliefs**

   Begin by writing down some of your core beliefs—about life, relationships, success, or any other areas that matter to you. Don't overthink; just jot down what feels true to you. These beliefs are part of the foundation of your voice and remind you of what you stand for.

2. **Track Moments of Self-Expression**

   Each day, note any moments when you expressed yourself honestly, whether it was a simple opinion, a feeling, or an idea you shared. How did it feel to speak up? Were you nervous or empowered? Tracking these moments helps you see the progress you're making in reclaiming your voice.

3. **Notice When You Hold Back**

   Pay attention to times when you wanted to speak up but held back. What stopped you? Was it fear, doubt, or worry about others' reactions? Writing about these moments can reveal patterns and help you identify situations where you may need extra encouragement to express yourself.

4. **Explore "I Statements"**

   Practice using "I statements" in your journal and daily life. Statements like "I think...," "I feel...," and "I believe..." ground your perspective in your personal truth. Writing these statements builds confidence in owning your opinions and feelings without apology.

5. **Reflect on What Your Voice Means to You**

   At the end of the week, take time to reflect on what it means to reclaim your voice. Write about how it feels to be more in touch with your authentic self-expression. What are you discovering about yourself? What do you want your voice to represent moving forward?

Final Thought

Reclaiming your voice is about more than speaking up; it's about reconnecting with who you are and having the courage to live in alignment with that truth. Your voice is a powerful tool, one that allows you to navigate life with purpose, clarity, and authenticity. When you trust your own voice, you're able to make decisions that reflect your values and pursue goals that resonate with your heart, rather than simply following others' expectations.

Remember, your voice matters not because it's the loudest, but because it's uniquely yours. Embrace your perspective, your feelings, and your beliefs, and trust that they are worthy of being expressed. The world may be loud, but within that noise, your voice has a place, a purpose, and a power all its own. Trust it, honor it, and let it guide you toward a life that feels truly yours. The journey to reclaiming your voice is one of the most freeing, empowering paths you'll ever walk.

CHAPTER 16

Aligning with Your Core Values

Core values are the guiding principles that ground and define you. They represent what truly matters to you, whether it's honesty, creativity, compassion, growth, freedom, or resilience. When you live in alignment with your values, you make choices that feel authentic and fulfilling, allowing you to navigate life with a sense of purpose. Your values act as a compass, pointing you toward actions, relationships, and goals that are in tune with who you genuinely are.

In a world where external expectations and distractions are everywhere, staying connected to your values can feel challenging. But when you know what you stand for, you're able to make decisions that honor your true self, even when the world pulls you in different directions. This chapter is about discovering, defining, and honoring your core values so that they can guide you toward a life that feels meaningful and uniquely yours.

How to Discover and Align with Your Core Values

Identifying your core values requires self-reflection, honesty, and a willingness to dig deep. Here are steps to help you clarify what truly matters to you and start aligning your life with those principles:

1. **Reflect on Moments of Fulfillment**

Think back to times in your life when you felt most fulfilled, proud, or connected. What were you doing, and why did it feel meaningful? Reflecting on these moments can reveal underlying values that were at play, such as kindness, achievement, curiosity, or community.

2. **Identify Your Top Values**

Make a list of values that resonate with you, then narrow it down to five to seven that feel most essential. These are the values that, when honored, bring you a sense of peace, purpose, and joy. Examples could include honesty, growth, balance, courage, or family.

3. **Define What Each Value Means to You**

Your values are unique, and how you define them may differ from others. For each core value, write a short description of what it means to you personally. This gives clarity and depth to each value, helping you see how it plays a role in your life.

4. **Evaluate Your Current Alignment**

Take an honest look at your life—your work, relationships, habits, and goals. Ask yourself if they reflect your values or if there are areas where you're feeling disconnected. This evaluation can help you identify areas to adjust so that your daily life aligns more closely with your true priorities.

5. **Use Values as a Decision-Making Tool**

When faced with a choice, ask yourself, "Does this align with my values?" Decisions that honor your values will feel more natural and energizing, while those that go against them may leave you feeling uneasy. Let your values guide you, especially in moments of doubt or uncertainty.

Weekly Exercise: Values in Action

This week, try a "Values in Action" exercise to explore how your core values can guide your daily choices and interactions. This exercise will help you create small but meaningful changes that bring your life closer in alignment with what truly matters to you.

1. **Write Down Your Top 5 Values**

   Begin by writing down the five core values that resonate most deeply with you. Keep them visible—on your phone, a sticky note, or in a journal—so they're a constant reminder of what matters to you.

2. **Identify One Area of Misalignment**

   Think of an area in your life where you feel misaligned with your values, like work, relationships, or self-care. Write down why it feels out of sync and which value(s) are lacking. This awareness helps you see where small changes can make a big difference.

3. **Set a Value-Based Intention**

   Choose one value to focus on this week and set an intention to live by it. For example, if one of your core values is creativity, set aside time to explore a creative hobby. Or if compassion is a value, practice active listening or acts of kindness. Setting an intention allows you to bring your values to life in practical, everyday ways.

4. **Reflect on Daily Decisions**

   Throughout the week, pause before making decisions—big or small—and ask yourself, "Does this choice honor my values?" Notice how it feels to make decisions that align with your true priorities. Small, value-based choices build confidence in living authentically.

5. **Journal About the Experience**

   At the end of the week, reflect in your journal on what you noticed. How did living in alignment with your values affect your mood, energy, or sense of fulfillment? Journaling about the experience helps reinforce the importance of your values as a guiding force.

Final Thought

Aligning with your core values isn't a one-time task—it's a lifelong practice. The more you honor your values, the stronger your sense of self becomes. Living by your values brings a sense of peace and purpose that can't be achieved by following others' expectations or pursuing goals that don't resonate with you. By letting your values guide your actions, you create a life that reflects who you truly are.

Remember, your values are not just ideals—they're the foundation of a fulfilling life. Let them guide your choices, relationships, and dreams. Embrace them fully, and you'll find that each step you take brings you closer to a life of authenticity, integrity, and purpose. In a world that often encourages compromise, living by your values is an act of courage and self-respect. Trust that your values will lead you where you're meant to go, creating a life that's uniquely and beautifully yours.

CHAPTER 17

The Wisdom of Intuition

Intuition is that subtle, inner sense that guides you without needing a full explanation. It's the voice that nudges you toward certain choices, warns you away from others, and often knows what's best for you before your mind fully catches up. In a world full of noise, opinions, and external advice, it's easy to ignore or question your intuition, especially when it conflicts with logic or with what others might think. But learning to trust your intuition is a powerful way to connect with your true self, make choices that feel right for you, and navigate life with confidence and authenticity.

This chapter is about recognizing, listening to, and trusting your own gut feelings. Your intuition is a valuable compass that often has your best interests at heart, even when it doesn't give you all the answers upfront. By strengthening this inner connection, you'll find that you can approach life's decisions with more ease, self-trust, and clarity.

How to Recognize and Trust Your Intuition

Trusting your intuition doesn't require a drastic shift. It's a gradual practice of tuning in and learning to distinguish it from fears, doubts, or external voices. Here are some steps to help you recognize and build trust in your own gut feelings:

1. **Notice Physical Sensations**
   Intuition often speaks through the body. You might feel a sense of calm, excitement, or lightness when something is right for you, or tension, unease, or heaviness when it's not. Start paying attention to these physical cues—your body often knows what your mind has yet to process.

2. **Practice Mindfulness to Quiet the Mind**
   When the mind is noisy, intuition can be harder to hear. Try practicing mindfulness, whether through meditation, deep breathing, or simply sitting quietly. Calming your mind allows you to tune in to subtle feelings and sensations, creating space for your intuition to come through more clearly.

3. **Reflect on Past Intuitive Moments**
   Think back to times when you had a gut feeling that proved to be accurate, even if you couldn't fully explain it. Write down a few of these moments and reflect on what they felt like. Recognizing patterns in how your intuition has helped you in the past builds confidence in trusting it now.

4. **Ask Yourself, "How Do I Really Feel About This?"**
   When faced with a decision, take a moment to tune into your emotions and ask, "How do I truly feel about this?" Focus on the initial feeling that arises before your mind starts to rationalize. Your first response often carries the truest answer from your intuition.

5. **Differentiate Intuition from Fear**
   Fear and intuition can feel similar, especially when they're telling you to avoid something. However, fear often feels tense, urgent, and anxiety-driven, while intuition tends to feel calm, even if it's nudging you toward something unexpected. If you're unsure, ask yourself if the feeling is based on past experiences or present guidance.

Weekly Exercise: The Intuition Journal

This week, try keeping an "Intuition Journal" to help you tune into and strengthen your intuitive abilities. This practice will help you become more aware of your gut feelings and how they influence your choices.

1. **Write Down Daily Intuitive Moments**

    Each day, jot down any moments when you had a gut feeling, even if it was small. It could be choosing a certain route, sensing someone's mood, or deciding on an unexpected action. This practice helps you recognize the role intuition plays in your daily life.

2. **Reflect on How It Felt**

    For each intuitive moment, describe how it felt in your body and mind. Did you feel calm or tense? Light or heavy? Getting familiar with how intuition feels helps you identify it more easily in the future.

3. **Practice One Intuitive Decision Each Day**

    Choose one small decision each day based purely on your gut feeling. It could be as simple as deciding what to eat, which way to go, or how to spend your time. Practicing small intuitive choices builds trust in your inner guidance.

4. **Record the Outcome**

    After acting on your intuition, write down what happened as a result. Did the choice feel aligned, peaceful, or rewarding? Recording outcomes helps reinforce trust in your intuition and highlights its positive influence.

5. **Reflect on a Larger Decision with Intuition**

    At the end of the week, think about a larger decision you're facing. Quiet your mind, tune into your inner voice, and ask yourself, "What feels right for me?" Trust whatever feeling arises, knowing that your intuition is here to support your growth.

Final Thought

Listening to your intuition is like reconnecting with an old friend—the more you nurture the relationship, the clearer and stronger it becomes. Your intuition is a powerful source of guidance, one that doesn't rely on logic or explanation but on a deeper understanding of what's best for you. By learning to trust this inner wisdom, you open the door to decisions that feel right, even when they don't make immediate sense to others.

Remember, your intuition is unique, as it's shaped by your life experiences, values, and dreams. Trust that it's here to help you stay true to yourself and lead you on the path that's meant for you. Embrace it, honor it, and know that you have within you a reliable compass guiding you toward choices that align with your authentic self. Let your intuition be your quiet strength, your ally in moments of uncertainty, and a reminder that you already have the answers you seek.

CHAPTER 18

Self-Compassion: Friend or Critic?

We all have an inner voice, one that can either build us up or tear us down. For many, this voice is often more critical than kind, quick to point out mistakes, doubts, and insecurities. This inner critic might feel like it's pushing you to improve or avoid mistakes, but in reality, constant self-criticism can undermine confidence, create stress, and make it harder to truly accept yourself. On the other hand, self-compassion—treating yourself with understanding and kindness—has the power to transform this voice from a harsh critic into a supportive friend. Self-compassion doesn't mean avoiding growth; it means approaching growth with kindness rather than judgment.

This chapter explores how to shift from self-criticism to self-compassion and create a more nurturing inner dialogue. When you practice self-compassion, you learn to treat yourself with the same understanding and support you would offer a friend, especially when things don't go as planned. This shift helps you build resilience, embrace imperfection, and create a foundation for personal growth rooted in self-acceptance.

How to Transform Self-Criticism into Self-Compassion

Turning self-criticism into self-compassion is a practice that requires patience and self-awareness. Here are some ways to start nurturing a kinder, more understanding inner dialogue:

1. **Notice the Voice of Self-Criticism**
   Begin by observing when and how self-criticism arises. Notice the words, tone, and emotions associated with it. Is there a specific situation that triggers it, like making a mistake, facing rejection, or feeling unprepared? Recognizing the voice of self-criticism is the first step to changing it.

2. **Ask, "Would I Say This to a Friend?"**
   When you catch yourself being self-critical, ask, "Would I say this to a friend in the same situation?" Chances are, you would be much kinder to them than you're being to yourself. Practicing this exercise reminds you to treat yourself with the same compassion you'd extend to someone you care about.

3. **Reframe Mistakes as Learning Opportunities**
   Instead of seeing mistakes as failures, try reframing them as valuable lessons. Self-compassionate thinking allows you to acknowledge errors without attaching judgment. Ask yourself, "What can I learn from this?" This mindset shift transforms mistakes into growth opportunities rather than reasons for self-criticism.

4. **Practice Self-Compassion Statements**
   Replace self-critical thoughts with self-compassionate statements, like "It's okay to struggle," "I'm allowed to make mistakes," or "I'm doing my best, and that's enough." These affirmations help soften the voice of the inner critic and allow you to be more gentle with yourself.

5. **Recognize Shared Humanity**
   Remind yourself that everyone experiences setbacks, self-doubt, and imperfect moments. You're not alone in your struggles;

they're part of the human experience. This understanding of shared humanity reduces feelings of isolation and helps you view your challenges with greater compassion.

Weekly Exercise: The Self-Compassion Journal

This week, try keeping a "Self-Compassion Journal" to transform your inner critic into a supportive friend. This exercise encourages reflection, reframing, and practicing kindness toward yourself.

1. **Identify Self-Critical Moments**
    Each day, write down moments when you felt self-critical. Describe what triggered the criticism and the words or thoughts that came to mind. This practice helps you observe patterns and recognize situations where self-compassion is needed most.

2. **Reframe with Self-Compassion**
    For each self-critical moment, rewrite the thought as a self-compassionate statement. For example, if you wrote, "I can't believe I messed that up," reframe it as, "It's okay to make mistakes; I can learn from this." Practicing this reframing shifts your mindset from judgment to understanding.

3. **List Three Acts of Kindness Toward Yourself**
    At the start of the week, choose three small acts of kindness to show yourself. These could be taking a break, treating yourself to a favorite meal, or setting aside time to do something you enjoy. By treating yourself kindly in small ways, you reinforce the practice of self-compassion.

4. **Practice Self-Compassionate Breathing**
    When self-criticism feels overwhelming, take a few minutes to breathe deeply and repeat a compassionate phrase, like "I am enough" or "I am worthy of kindness." This mindful breathing exercise helps you calm your mind, offering a break from the inner critic and reconnecting you to a sense of peace.

5. **Reflect on Your Week with Gratitude**
    At the end of the week, reflect on your self-compassion journey. What moments felt lighter when you practiced kindness toward yourself? Write down any positive changes you noticed in your mood, confidence, or energy. Gratitude for these shifts reinforces the benefits of self-compassion.

Final Thought

Self-compassion is a skill that grows with practice. Each time you choose understanding over judgment, you strengthen a foundation of kindness that helps you weather life's challenges with grace and resilience. When you treat yourself with compassion, you foster a relationship of trust, patience, and support within yourself.

Remember, you deserve the same gentleness and encouragement that you would offer a friend or loved one. When you become your own ally, you give yourself the freedom to learn, grow, and navigate life without the weight of harsh self-criticism. Embrace self-compassion as a way to support your growth from a place of self-acceptance rather than pressure or perfectionism.

Trust that you're enough as you are, flaws and all. With self-compassion as your inner guide, you'll find a source of strength and peace that allows you to approach life's ups and downs with a kind, resilient heart. Let self-compassion be the voice that reminds you: you're worthy of love and understanding—especially from yourself.

CHAPTER 19

The Weight of Old Labels

Throughout our lives, we often pick up labels, some given by others and some that we create ourselves. These labels might have once helped us understand who we were or how we fit into the world, but over time, they can start to feel restrictive or outdated. Labels like "the shy one," "the responsible one," or "the troublemaker" can cling to us, even when we've outgrown them. Sometimes, old labels create pressure to keep acting in certain ways or reinforce limiting beliefs about what we're capable of.

Releasing these past labels is an act of self-liberation. It's about letting go of definitions that no longer resonate with who you are today and allowing yourself the freedom to evolve without feeling bound by outdated expectations. This chapter explores how to recognize and release the labels that no longer define you so you can create space for growth, self-acceptance, and new possibilities.

How to Release Old Labels

Letting go of past labels isn't about rejecting parts of your past; it's about recognizing how you've grown and embracing a fuller version of yourself. Here are some steps to help you identify and release old labels that may be holding you back:

1. **Reflect on Labels You've Carried**
    Think about labels that you've been given or that you've placed on yourself. Write them down, and consider where each label came from. Was it something someone called you, a role you filled, or a way you coped in certain situations? Understanding their origin helps you see how these labels took shape.

2. **Acknowledge Why They No Longer Fit**
    For each label, ask yourself if it still resonates with who you are today. If it feels restrictive, ask, "Why doesn't this label fit anymore?" Maybe you've developed new strengths, grown beyond old habits, or gained experiences that have reshaped your identity. Acknowledging this growth allows you to see how much you've evolved.

3. **Replace Labels with Descriptions**
    Instead of labeling yourself, try describing who you are with phrases that feel open and dynamic. For example, replace "the shy one" with "someone who enjoys thoughtful conversations." Descriptions allow for flexibility, giving you space to embrace all aspects of yourself without feeling confined to one definition.

4. **Challenge Limiting Beliefs Tied to Labels**
    Old labels often carry limiting beliefs. If you've labeled yourself as "not creative" or "the serious one," you may be holding yourself back from exploring other qualities. Ask yourself, "What would I try if I didn't believe this label?" Challenge yourself to explore new interests and perspectives that defy these outdated labels.

5. **Embrace the Freedom to Change**
    Give yourself permission to change and grow without needing a label to define you. Embracing your fluidity and complexity allows you to feel comfortable shifting directions, pursuing new interests, and becoming the fullest version of yourself. Remind yourself that you are not limited by any single word or definition.

Weekly Exercise: Label Liberation Journal

This week, try a "Label Liberation Journal" exercise to help you identify, examine, and release past labels. This practice encourages self-reflection, self-acceptance, and the freedom to redefine who you are.

1. **List Old Labels You're Ready to Release**

    Write down the labels that no longer feel true or helpful to you. These might be things like "the perfectionist," "the people-pleaser," or "the black sheep." Seeing these labels on paper gives you the clarity to assess them and understand their impact on your self-perception.

2. **Write About How They Shaped You**

    For each label, write a few sentences about how it shaped your choices, behavior, or self-image. Did the label influence the way you acted or held yourself back? Reflecting on this allows you to understand how labels may have played a role in your past without defining your future.

3. **Describe Who You Are Without These Labels**

    Take time to imagine and describe yourself free of these labels. Write statements that reflect your true, evolving self, such as "I am open to new experiences," or "I am both responsible and adventurous." This reframing helps you create a self-image that's flexible and open to growth.

4. **Practice One Action Outside Your Old Labels**

    Challenge yourself to do something that defies one of your old labels. If you were labeled "the shy one," try speaking up in a small group. If you were seen as "the serious one," embrace a playful activity. Taking one action outside your label empowers you to expand beyond those old definitions.

5. **Write a Letter of Gratitude and Release**

    At the end of the week, write a letter to the labels you're ready to let go of. Thank them for any role they played in your life, but gently release them. Acknowledge that while they were once part of your story, they no longer define you. Letting go with gratitude helps you move forward with compassion for your past.

Final Thought

Releasing old labels is an act of freedom. It's about allowing yourself the space to grow, change, and redefine who you are without carrying outdated expectations. You're a complex, evolving person, and no single label can capture the depth of your experiences, dreams, and potential. By letting go of these labels, you open yourself up to new ways of being, giving yourself the flexibility to become whoever you choose to be.

Remember, you're not bound by your past or by any one definition. Embrace the richness of who you are and give yourself permission to explore new qualities, roles, and interests. Trust that you are so much more than any label could ever contain. With each step you take away from restrictive labels, you move closer to living as your true, multifaceted self—free, dynamic, and open to all that life has to offer.

CHAPTER 20

Why Showing Up Matters

In a world full of distractions, demands, and competing priorities, showing up for ourselves can sometimes feel like the hardest thing to do. Whether it's committing to a goal, nurturing a passion, or simply following through on a promise to take care of yourself, showing up is a powerful way to build self-trust and stay true to your own journey. It's a practice of honoring your path, even on days when motivation is low, and progress feels slow.

Showing up isn't about perfection or achieving everything right away; it's about consistently choosing to take small steps toward your growth and well-being. This chapter explores how to build a habit of self-commitment, so you can show up for yourself and stay connected to your goals, values, and dreams. By developing this habit, you'll strengthen your ability to follow through, trust yourself, and create a life that feels purposeful and aligned.

How to Build a Habit of Self-Commitment

Showing up for yourself is about creating sustainable habits that reflect your values and priorities. Here are some steps to help you cultivate a strong habit of self-commitment:

1. **Define What Showing Up Means to You**

   Take a moment to reflect on what "showing up" means in your life. Is it dedicating time to a creative passion, following a health routine, setting boundaries, or simply being present with loved ones? Defining what showing up looks like for you gives clarity to your efforts and helps you set intentions that feel meaningful.

2. **Set Realistic, Small Goals**

   Start with small, achievable goals that build confidence in your ability to follow through. Instead of committing to big, overwhelming goals, break them down into smaller steps that you can work on daily or weekly. Consistency in these small actions creates momentum and reinforces the habit of showing up.

3. **Create Routines That Support You**

   Routines make it easier to show up, even on days when motivation is low. If you want to build a habit of self-care, for example, set up a morning or evening routine that includes moments of quiet reflection or activities you enjoy. Routines become anchors that make showing up feel natural, even when life gets busy.

4. **Hold Yourself Accountable with Compassion**

   Self-commitment doesn't mean rigid discipline. It means gently holding yourself accountable while also allowing room for self-compassion. If you miss a day or fall short, don't dwell on it or judge yourself. Instead, remind yourself why you started and refocus on the next opportunity to show up.

5. **Celebrate Small Wins Along the Way**

   Every time you show up, celebrate it, no matter how small it may seem. Recognize the progress you're making, even if it's just taking one small step forward. Celebrating these moments builds positive reinforcement, helping you associate showing up with feelings of accomplishment and pride.

Weekly Exercise: The Show-Up Tracker

This week, try a "Show-Up Tracker" exercise to build consistency and keep yourself connected to the habit of self-commitment. This exercise will help you recognize the power of small steps and celebrate each instance of showing up.

1. **Set One Daily Goal**

    Choose one small goal to focus on each day, like spending ten minutes journaling, practicing a skill, or dedicating time to an important project. Keep it simple and achievable. The goal is to build the habit of showing up, not to overwhelm yourself.

2. **Create a Visual Tracker**

    Use a calendar, notebook, or app to track each day you complete your daily goal. Check off each day or add a small symbol that represents your progress. Seeing your efforts visually reinforces your commitment and builds pride in showing up consistently.

3. **Reflect on the Experience of Showing Up**

    At the end of each day, take a few moments to reflect on how it felt to show up for yourself. Did you feel more accomplished, grounded, or motivated? Recognizing the impact of showing up strengthens your desire to keep the habit alive.

4. **Adjust When Needed, but Keep Going**

    Some days may feel harder than others, and that's okay. If you need to adjust your goal or skip a day, practice self-compassion and refocus on the next day. Showing up is about consistency, not perfection, and every small step counts.

5. **Celebrate the Week's Progress**

    At the end of the week, celebrate your commitment. Reflect on any positive shifts you noticed and take pride in each instance you followed through. Whether it's one day or all seven, acknowledging your efforts helps you appreciate the power of showing up and motivates you to continue.

Final Thought

Showing up is an art, one that becomes easier with practice and patience. By committing to small, intentional steps, you create a foundation of self-trust and build a habit of following through, even when challenges arise. Each time you show up, you reinforce the belief that you are capable, resilient, and dedicated to your growth.

Remember, showing up isn't about doing it all or doing it perfectly. It's about being there for yourself in ways that matter, honoring your goals, and choosing progress over perfection. Trust that each small step you take is moving you closer to a life that feels true and fulfilling.

As you continue on this journey, let the habit of showing up be a reminder of your own strength, dedication, and commitment to living authentically. Every time you choose to show up, you're choosing to invest in yourself, your dreams, and the person you're becoming. Embrace this habit as an expression of self-love, knowing that you're building a path that's uniquely yours, one step at a time.

Living Authentically in the World

CHAPTER 21

The Power of Speaking Your Truth

In relationships, work, and social interactions, the ability to share your truth—your beliefs, needs, and feelings—honestly and openly is a profound expression of authenticity. Yet, sharing your truth can feel vulnerable. You might worry about being misunderstood, judged, or rejected. But when you express who you are with honesty and kindness, you strengthen connections, build trust, and honor your true self.

Sharing your truth doesn't mean imposing your views or constantly explaining yourself. Instead, it's about communicating your needs and beliefs with respect and empathy, giving others a window into who you really are. This chapter explores how to express yourself genuinely, with a balance of honesty and compassion, so you can build connections that reflect the real you.

How to Share Your Truth with Honesty and Kindness

Sharing your truth is about expressing yourself in a way that feels authentic while honoring the feelings and perspectives of others. Here are some steps to help you communicate your truth with clarity, openness, and compassion:

1. **Know Your Truth Before You Share It**

Before sharing, take a moment to understand your feelings, needs, or beliefs. Ask yourself, "What am I really feeling?" and "Why is this important to me?" Clarity helps you express yourself more effectively and ensures that what you share is genuinely your truth, not a reaction to external pressure or expectations.

2. **Choose Words that Reflect Honesty and Kindness**

Honest communication doesn't have to be harsh. Think about how you can express your thoughts in a way that respects both your own truth and the other person's feelings. Using "I" statements, like "I feel" or "I believe," makes it easier to share your perspective without sounding accusatory or defensive.

3. **Be Clear and Direct**

When expressing your truth, aim for simplicity and clarity. Avoid downplaying your thoughts or over-explaining, as this can dilute your message. Instead, communicate directly and concisely. Clear, straightforward communication leaves less room for misunderstandings and reinforces the importance of your truth.

4. **Listen with Openness**

Sharing your truth is a two-way street. Once you've expressed yourself, be willing to listen openly to the other person's response. Even if they don't fully agree, listening allows space for understanding and mutual respect. Compassionate listening also encourages others to honor their own truth, strengthening the connection between you.

5. **Accept Differences with Respect**

Not everyone will share or fully understand your truth, and that's okay. Part of authentic expression is recognizing that each person has their own unique perspective. Respectfully acknowledging differences allows you to stay true to yourself without expecting complete agreement from others.

Weekly Exercise: The Truth Sharing Journal

This week, try a "Truth Sharing Journal" exercise to explore and practice expressing yourself with honesty and kindness. This exercise will help you reflect on your truths and build confidence in sharing them with others.

1. **Identify a Truth You'd Like to Share**
    Begin by identifying a truth that you'd like to express. It could be an opinion, a feeling, a boundary, or a personal experience. Write it down, and reflect on why it feels important to share. Understanding the significance of your truth helps you connect more deeply with it.

2. **Choose How You'd Like to Express It**
    Think about the person or people with whom you'd like to share this truth. Consider the best way to communicate it, whether in person, through a written note, or even as a voice message. Choose an approach that feels comfortable and that you believe will allow for open, honest communication.

3. **Write Your Truth as an "I Statement"**
    Before you share, try writing your truth as an "I statement," such as, "I feel...," "I believe...," or "I need..." This helps ground your message in your perspective and keeps the focus on your own experience, reducing the risk of misunderstandings or defensive responses.

4. **Reflect on How It Feels to Share**
    After expressing your truth, write down any feelings that arose. Did you feel relief, pride, or vulnerability? Reflecting on these emotions helps you build self-awareness and learn from each experience of sharing authentically.

5. **Celebrate Your Courage to Be Real**
    Acknowledge yourself for having the courage to express your truth. Recognize that each time you do this, you're strengthening

your ability to live authentically. Small celebrations of this courage help you feel proud of your growth and reinforce the habit of sharing your truth.

Final Thought

Sharing your truth with honesty and kindness is a powerful way to honor yourself and create genuine connections. It allows you to show up as you are, without feeling the need to hide or mold yourself to others' expectations. When you express your truth respectfully, you invite others to do the same, creating a space where authenticity is welcomed and valued.

Remember, sharing your truth isn't about proving yourself or persuading others. It's about standing in your own experience, giving voice to what matters to you, and trusting that your perspective is worthy of being heard. The courage to share your truth will bring you closer to a life that feels real, free, and aligned with who you are.

Embrace the art of honest, kind expression, knowing that each truth you share is a step toward deeper self-acceptance and more meaningful connections. Trust that the real you is enough and that your truth deserves to be heard. In sharing who you are, you're building a life that reflects your authentic self—bravely, gently, and wholeheartedly.

CHAPTER 22

The Freedom to Define Success for Yourself

Success is often portrayed as a one-size-fits-all journey—a linear path of achievements that includes career milestones, social status, material wealth, and constant productivity. Society's definition of success can feel like a checklist that, once completed, supposedly brings happiness and fulfillment. But success isn't truly meaningful if it's based on someone else's values and not your own. Real success is personal, rooted in what matters most to you, and aligned with the life you want to create.

Redefining success means moving beyond external definitions and embracing a version of success that reflects your unique values, aspirations, and lifestyle. This chapter is about breaking free from traditional expectations and discovering what success looks like for *you*. When you define success on your own terms, it becomes a source of fulfillment, not pressure, and brings you closer to a life that feels balanced and authentic.

How to Redefine Success Based on Your Values

Creating a personal definition of success requires introspection and a willingness to challenge societal norms. Here are steps to help you redefine success in a way that feels aligned with your values and vision for life:

1. **Reflect on What Success Means to You**
    Begin by asking yourself, "What does success look like for me?" Think about moments when you felt truly fulfilled or proud. Success might not mean climbing a career ladder or accumulating wealth; it could mean having meaningful relationships, living a balanced life, creating something valuable, or pursuing personal growth.

2. **Identify Your Core Values**
    Values are the foundation of authentic success. Identify three to five core values—such as creativity, connection, freedom, health, or contribution—that resonate with you. Use these values as your compass to guide what success means to you, so that your goals feel both achievable and meaningful.

3. **Let Go of Societal Expectations**
    Success as defined by society may not align with your personal goals, and that's okay. Give yourself permission to let go of any pressure to meet external standards, whether they come from family, friends, or social media. Remember that success is not about meeting others' expectations; it's about living a life that feels true to who you are.

4. **Create Success Goals That Reflect Your Values**
    Think about goals that would make you feel successful based on your values. For example, if connection is a core value, success might mean building strong relationships and spending quality time with loved ones. If creativity is a value, it might mean dedicating time to pursue an artistic passion. Defining success goals based on your values makes each accomplishment feel personally rewarding.

5. **Practice Gratitude for Your Own Path**
    Embracing your unique path of success requires gratitude for the

steps you're taking, no matter how different they may look from others. Practice gratitude for each milestone, lesson, and choice that aligns with your vision of success. This habit helps you stay grounded in your journey and focus on what truly matters to you.

Weekly Exercise: The Personal Success Journal

This week, try a "Personal Success Journal" exercise to help you explore and redefine success on your own terms. This practice encourages reflection, clarity, and appreciation for a path that feels uniquely yours.

1. **Describe Your Ideal Vision of Success**
Take a few minutes to imagine what an ideal version of success looks like for you. Write down what comes to mind, whether it's a balanced life, meaningful work, close relationships, or continuous learning. This vision serves as your guide, helping you prioritize what's most important.

2. **List Core Values That Define Your Success**
Write down three to five values that resonate with you, and describe how each value influences your idea of success. For example, if one of your values is freedom, you might define success as having control over your schedule. This clarity keeps your success goals aligned with your true self.

3. **Identify "Success Myths" You're Ready to Release**
Think about common success myths that don't serve you, like "success means working 24/7" or "I need to be wealthy to be successful." Write these myths down and consciously decide to let them go. Releasing these myths frees you from unrealistic expectations and gives you room to create a success path that's authentic.

4. **Set One Value-Based Success Goal for the Week**
Choose a small, achievable goal that aligns with one of your core

values. For instance, if personal growth is a value, commit to reading a book on a topic you're curious about. Completing value-based goals helps you build a habit of working toward success in a way that feels fulfilling.

5. **Celebrate Milestones Along Your Path**

At the end of the week, reflect on any progress, insights, or positive shifts that you experienced. Celebrate even the smallest steps, knowing that they're part of your unique success journey. Recognizing these milestones reinforces your confidence and motivation to continue on your path.

Final Thought

Redefining success is about honoring your true self, embracing your values, and allowing your journey to be uniquely yours. When you break free from society's standards, you create a version of success that resonates with your life, one that brings you joy, fulfillment, and peace. Success becomes not just an end goal but a way of living that feels deeply satisfying and authentic.

Remember, success doesn't have to look like anyone else's, and it's not measured by how well you keep up with external expectations. True success is found in the choices, values, and relationships that make your life meaningful to you. Trust your inner compass, honor your own pace, and celebrate each step of your journey as it unfolds.

As you redefine success on your terms, know that you're creating a life that reflects who you are at your core. Embrace this journey with confidence and gratitude, knowing that every step you take toward your own vision of success brings you closer to a life that feels truly rewarding, purposeful, and complete.

CHAPTER 23

Relationships as Mirrors

Our relationships—whether with friends, family, romantic partners, or colleagues—offer us more than companionship; they act as mirrors, reflecting back aspects of who we are. Through relationships, we get a clearer view of our strengths, weaknesses, values, and beliefs. Each interaction provides insights into our inner selves, showing us where we feel confident, where we need healing, and what we truly want. Relationships can reveal parts of us we may not fully see or understand, helping us grow by offering a lens into our character, behaviors, and emotional responses.

When we approach relationships as mirrors, they become opportunities for self-discovery and transformation. This chapter is about recognizing how relationships reflect parts of ourselves and how we can use these reflections to grow. By paying attention to what we see in our interactions with others, we gain insight into our own patterns, learn to cultivate healthier relationships, and embrace growth in new and meaningful ways.

How Relationships Reflect Who You Are

Relationships hold up a mirror to different parts of your life, both positive and challenging. Here are some ways relationships reveal truths about you and support your journey of growth:

1. **Notice Emotional Triggers**

Pay attention to moments when you feel triggered, whether by frustration, jealousy, anger, or hurt. Emotional triggers often highlight unresolved issues or insecurities within us. Instead of focusing on the other person's actions, ask yourself, "Why did this affect me so deeply?" Understanding triggers helps you see where healing and self-compassion are needed.

2. **Observe Patterns in Behavior**

Relationships often reveal patterns in how we communicate, show affection, or respond to conflict. Do you notice recurring dynamics, like being overly accommodating or avoiding confrontation? Recognizing these patterns is the first step to breaking cycles that no longer serve you, allowing you to approach relationships in healthier ways.

3. **Identify Qualities You Admire in Others**

The qualities you admire in others—like kindness, confidence, or humor—often reflect traits you value in yourself or aspire to develop. Appreciating these qualities can inspire you to nurture them within. Conversely, traits you dislike in others may mirror unresolved parts of yourself that you're ready to work on or understand better.

4. **Recognize Boundaries Through Discomfort**

When you feel discomfort or resistance in relationships, it can be a sign that a boundary has been crossed or needs to be established. Use these moments as cues to define your personal boundaries. By respecting and communicating your limits, you create healthier, more balanced connections with others.

5. **Reflect on Feedback from Trusted People**

Sometimes, those closest to us offer insights that we may not see on our own. Constructive feedback from people who genuinely care about you can be a valuable mirror, reflecting areas for personal growth. Approach this feedback with an open mind, using it as an opportunity to understand yourself more deeply and make positive changes.

Weekly Exercise: The Relationship Reflection Journal

This week, try a "Relationship Reflection Journal" exercise to explore how your relationships reflect who you are and reveal areas for growth. This practice will help you become more mindful of the lessons and insights your relationships provide.

1. **Identify a Relationship or Situation to Reflect On**
   Choose one recent interaction that brought up strong emotions or revealed something new about yourself. It could be a conversation with a friend, a disagreement with family, or a moment of closeness with a partner. Writing about this specific experience helps bring clarity to the reflection.

2. **Explore Emotional Reactions**
   Write down any strong emotions you felt during or after the interaction. Ask yourself, "What about this moment brought up these emotions?" Reflecting on your reactions helps you understand what might be behind your feelings and what this relationship is mirroring back to you.

3. **Look for Patterns and Insights**
   Consider whether this situation reflects a larger pattern in your relationships, like a tendency to avoid expressing needs or a habit of putting others first. If a pattern emerges, note it down. Recognizing patterns helps you see areas for growth and choose new, healthier ways to engage in relationships.

4. **Identify Qualities that Resonate**
   Think about the qualities that stood out to you in the other person—positive or negative. Do these qualities reflect something you aspire to develop in yourself or something you'd like to re-

lease? This reflection reveals values you want to nurture or areas you're ready to transform.

5. **Write Down One Insight to Apply Moving Forward**
Based on your reflections, choose one insight to carry with you. It could be a reminder to set a boundary, an affirmation of a quality you want to nurture, or an intention to respond differently in similar situations. Applying insights helps you grow through your relationships, using them as tools for self-awareness and positive change.

Final Thought

Seeing relationships as mirrors transforms every connection into an opportunity for growth. By looking at what others reflect back to you, you gain a deeper understanding of your inner world—your beliefs, values, wounds, and strengths. This insight empowers you to make changes that align with your true self and create more authentic, fulfilling relationships.

Remember, relationships are not just about finding people who make you feel good; they're also about learning and evolving together. Some relationships may challenge you, while others bring out your best qualities. Both types serve a purpose on your path of self-discovery. Embrace each relationship as a chance to see yourself more clearly and grow into the person you want to become.

As you move forward, let relationships be your mirror. Trust that each interaction, whether smooth or challenging, has something valuable to teach you. Approach your connections with openness, curiosity, and a willingness to learn, knowing that each reflection is helping you become a truer, wiser, and more compassionate version of yourself.

CHAPTER 24

The Strength in Vulnerability

In a world that often equates strength with stoicism and independence, vulnerability might seem like a risk. Opening up, sharing your true feelings, and letting others see you without a mask can feel uncomfortable—even intimidating. But vulnerability is not a weakness; it's a powerful strength that fosters authentic connection, builds trust, and deepens our relationships. When you embrace vulnerability, you show up fully as yourself, inviting others to do the same. It's an act of courage that says, "I am willing to be seen as I am, flaws and all."

Embracing vulnerability means letting go of the need to appear perfect or in control and instead choosing authenticity. This chapter explores how to open up and share who you are with honesty and courage, creating space for meaningful connection and self-acceptance. By allowing yourself to be seen without fear, you step into a fuller, more connected version of yourself and experience relationships on a deeper, more rewarding level.

How to Embrace Vulnerability

Embracing vulnerability is a gradual practice of self-trust and openness. Here are some steps to help you feel more comfortable with being vulnerable in your relationships and everyday life:

1. **Acknowledge What Makes You Feel Vulnerable**
Start by identifying situations or topics that make you feel vulnerable, like sharing your dreams, admitting mistakes, or expressing your fears. Acknowledging these moments helps you understand what vulnerability means to you and where you can begin to lean into it with more openness.

2. **Reframe Vulnerability as Courage**
Remind yourself that vulnerability is not about exposing weakness—it's about embracing courage. Each time you allow yourself to be vulnerable, you're choosing to show up fully as you are, even if it feels risky. Viewing vulnerability as courage helps you see it as an empowering choice rather than something to avoid.

3. **Start Small with Safe People**
Practicing vulnerability doesn't mean sharing your deepest secrets right away. Begin by opening up in small ways with people you trust, like expressing an opinion, sharing a personal story, or admitting when you need help. These small acts of vulnerability build your confidence and help you feel safer being open with others.

4. **Focus on Authentic Connection, Not Approval**
Vulnerability is about creating genuine connection, not seeking approval. When you share openly, let your goal be to express your truth rather than trying to control how others respond. This mindset shift allows you to let go of perfectionism and embrace the freedom that comes from showing up as you are.

5. **Practice Self-Compassion When Vulnerability Feels Scary**
Being vulnerable can bring up feelings of fear, shame, or insecurity. When this happens, practice self-compassion by reminding yourself that it's okay to feel vulnerable. Treat yourself kindly, just as you would a friend who's taking a brave step. Self-compassion helps you embrace vulnerability without feeling overwhelmed by it.

Weekly Exercise: The Vulnerability Journal

This week, try keeping a "Vulnerability Journal" to explore moments of openness and reflect on how they make you feel. This exercise encourages gradual steps toward vulnerability, allowing you to experience its benefits in a safe, supportive way.

1. **Identify a Moment of Vulnerability Each Day**
    At the end of each day, write down a moment when you allowed yourself to be vulnerable. It could be a small act, like sharing a personal story with a friend, expressing an emotion, or trying something new that felt a bit uncomfortable. This practice helps you recognize and celebrate small acts of openness.

2. **Reflect on How It Felt to Be Vulnerable**
    For each moment, note how it felt to be vulnerable. Did you feel relief, fear, connection, or growth? Reflecting on these emotions allows you to understand your relationship with vulnerability and helps you see the courage in your actions.

3. **Describe Any Positive Outcomes**
    Did being vulnerable lead to a meaningful conversation, deeper connection, or a sense of self-acceptance? Write down any positive outcomes, no matter how small. Recognizing these moments helps reinforce the value of vulnerability and encourages you to keep opening up.

4. **Challenge Yourself to Share a Little More**
    Each day, think of one small way you can push yourself to be a bit more open. It could be expressing a feeling you usually keep hidden, sharing a dream you have, or admitting when you're struggling. These small steps build confidence and show you that vulnerability is not as scary as it seems.

5. **Reflect on Self-Compassion in Vulnerability**
    At the end of the week, write a short reflection on how you practiced self-compassion in moments of vulnerability. Were there

times you felt insecure or exposed? How did you respond to those feelings? Practicing kindness toward yourself strengthens your ability to embrace vulnerability with confidence.

Final Thought

Embracing vulnerability is a journey of self-acceptance, honesty, and courage. Each time you open up, you give others permission to do the same, creating a space of mutual trust and connection. Vulnerability allows you to experience life more fully, connecting with others in ways that are real, meaningful, and lasting.

Remember, vulnerability is not about being fearless—it's about choosing to show up, even when fear is present. It's about valuing authenticity over perfection and connection over self-protection. When you embrace vulnerability, you allow yourself to be seen, heard, and accepted as you are.

Trust that vulnerability will lead you to deeper connections, greater self-acceptance, and a more genuine life. Let go of the need to have it all together, and instead, let yourself be fully present in each moment, flaws and all. With vulnerability, you'll find a strength that isn't about hiding but about shining as your true self. Embrace it, honor it, and let it be the path that leads you closer to others and to the truest version of you.

CHAPTER 25

Courage in Being Different

In a world that often encourages conformity, it can feel challenging to stand out or embrace the qualities that make you different. Society frequently rewards people who fit into certain molds, which can create pressure to downplay the things that make you unique. But being different is a strength. Your individuality—the qualities, quirks, perspectives, and passions that make you *you*—is what brings color, creativity, and new ideas into the world. Having the courage to be different is about embracing these parts of yourself and celebrating them instead of hiding them.

This chapter is about finding the courage to stand out, honoring your unique qualities, and letting them shine without fear. By embracing your individuality, you free yourself from expectations, build self-confidence, and create a life that reflects your true self. This journey isn't just about self-acceptance; it's about seeing your uniqueness as a gift that deserves to be celebrated.

How to Celebrate Your Unique Qualities

Celebrating your individuality involves shifting your mindset, building self-confidence, and taking pride in the parts of yourself that stand out. Here are some ways to embrace and honor what makes you different:

1. **Identify What Makes You Unique**
   Start by recognizing the qualities, talents, and passions that set you apart. What do you love that others may not understand? What talents or interests do you have that are uniquely yours? Write these down and reflect on how they make you special. Knowing and appreciating what makes you different is the first step to embracing it.

2. **Challenge the Need for Approval**
   It's natural to want approval, but relying on it can make it hard to show up authentically. Challenge yourself to prioritize self-acceptance over external validation. Remind yourself that you don't need others' approval to embrace your true self. This practice allows you to celebrate your individuality without worrying about fitting in.

3. **Express Yourself Authentically**
   Embrace opportunities to express yourself in ways that feel true to you, whether through your personal style, creative projects, hobbies, or beliefs. Authentic expression helps you connect with who you are and builds confidence in showing up as your true self. The more you express your individuality, the easier it becomes to celebrate it.

4. **Focus on Your Strengths, Not Comparisons**
   When you feel different, it's easy to compare yourself to others and question your path. Instead, focus on your unique strengths and qualities. Remember that your differences add value, bringing new perspectives and experiences that others may not have. Shifting from comparison to self-appreciation helps you build pride in who you are.

5. **Connect with Like-Minded People**
   Surrounding yourself with people who celebrate individuality can make it easier to embrace your own. Seek out friends, communities, or groups that appreciate and encourage uniqueness.

When you're supported by others who value authenticity, you feel more empowered to be yourself without hiding.

Weekly Exercise: The "Celebrate Your Unique Self" Journal

This week, try a "Celebrate Your Unique Self" journal exercise to explore and honor the qualities that make you different. This practice helps you build confidence in your individuality and allows you to embrace it more fully.

1. **Write Down Your Unique Qualities**
   Begin by listing three to five qualities or interests that make you unique. These could be traits like creativity, curiosity, resilience, or unconventional interests. Write about why each one matters to you and how it brings something special to your life.

2. **Describe a Time You Felt Different**
   Think back to a time when you felt different or out of place because of one of your unique qualities. Describe the experience, and reflect on how it made you feel. This helps you see that being different isn't a weakness, but rather a part of what makes you interesting and valuable.

3. **Celebrate a Unique Achievement**
   Write about an achievement or experience that highlights your individuality. It could be a creative project, an unconventional path you pursued, or a time you stepped out of your comfort zone. Reflect on how this experience strengthened your confidence and allowed you to honor your true self.

4. **Set a Goal to Express Yourself Authentically**
   Choose one small way to express your unique qualities this week. It could be sharing a passion with someone, embracing a hobby you've been hiding, or trying a style that feels like you. Each step toward authentic self-expression strengthens your courage to be different.

5. **Reflect on How It Feels to Be Authentic**
At the end of the week, write about how it felt to show up authentically. Did you feel more confident, connected, or free? Recognizing these positive feelings helps reinforce the courage to continue embracing your uniqueness.

Final Thought

Having the courage to be different is about honoring your individuality and recognizing the value in your unique perspective. The world needs diverse voices, new ideas, and people who are unafraid to be themselves. When you embrace your differences, you not only enrich your own life but also inspire others to do the same.

Remember, authenticity is a strength, not a flaw. Embrace what makes you different with pride, knowing that your individuality is a gift that deserves to be celebrated. Each time you choose to be yourself, you break free from the pressure to conform and step into a life that feels true, fulfilling, and vibrant.

Trust that the parts of you that stand out are the very things that make you shine. Embrace your uniqueness, find joy in your individuality, and let your courage to be different lead you toward a life that feels genuinely yours. The journey to authenticity may not always be easy, but it is undoubtedly one of the most rewarding paths you can take.

Mindful Social Media

Social media can be a fantastic tool for connection, creativity, and discovery. But it can also create pressure to compare, conform, and project a version of ourselves that isn't entirely true. The endless scrolling, highlight reels, and filtered images can gradually influence how we see ourselves, sometimes pulling us away from our authentic values and creating a loop of comparison and validation-seeking.

Practicing mindful social media use helps you engage online in a way that feels balanced, purposeful, and true to who you are. By being intentional about how, when, and why you use social media, you can stay grounded in your values, avoid the traps of comparison, and create a digital space that uplifts rather than drains you.

How to Engage on Social Media Mindfully

Mindful social media use involves setting boundaries, staying aware of your intentions, and focusing on authenticity. Here are some ways to keep your social media experience aligned with your true self:

1. **Define Your Purpose for Using Social Media**
   Start by asking yourself why you use social media. Is it to connect with friends, find inspiration, share creativity, or stay informed? Defining your purpose allows you to use social media with inten-

tion, helping you focus on activities that genuinely support and enrich your life.

2. **Curate Who You Follow Based on Values**

Be mindful of who you follow and the types of content you regularly see. Follow people, brands, and pages that align with your values, inspire you, or support your well-being. Don't hesitate to unfollow accounts that make you feel pressured to conform, spark insecurity, or distract you from your goals.

3. **Set Boundaries for Time and Energy**

Create specific boundaries around your social media use to prevent mindless scrolling. Set daily or weekly limits, or designate certain times of the day to check your accounts. By placing boundaries around when and how much you engage, you protect your time and energy for things that are meaningful to you.

4. **Practice Mindful Scrolling and Posting**

Instead of rushing through your feed, pause to notice how each post makes you feel. When you come across content that triggers insecurity or comparison, remind yourself that social media is often a highlight reel and not the whole picture. And when you post, focus on sharing what feels authentic rather than seeking likes or validation.

5. **Be Intentional About Engagement**

Engage online with purpose by interacting with content that genuinely resonates with you. Leave comments that are meaningful, reach out to friends, or share content that feels uplifting or inspiring. Mindful engagement helps you stay connected to your community in an authentic way and strengthens positive online interactions.

Weekly Exercise: The Mindful Social Media Tracker

This week, try using a "Mindful Social Media Tracker" to help you reflect on your online habits and stay grounded in your values. This exercise encourages self-awareness, intention, and healthier social media practices.

1. **Define Your Social Media Goals**

   Write down three goals for your social media use this week. For example, you might decide to only spend 20 minutes a day on social media, limit your interactions to positive content, or post authentically without worrying about engagement metrics. These goals help you stay intentional and mindful in your online habits.

2. **Track Your Emotions While Scrolling**

   As you scroll, take note of how different content makes you feel. Write down any instances where you felt inspired, connected, stressed, or insecure. Recognizing these emotional triggers helps you understand how social media affects your mood and gives you insight into which content aligns with your well-being.

3. **Reflect on Your Online Persona**

   Think about the version of yourself you present online. Does it feel true to who you are? Write down what feels authentic about your social media presence and what might feel curated or filtered. Reflecting on this helps you post more authentically and build a presence that represents the real you.

4. **Engage Meaningfully**

   Each day, challenge yourself to engage meaningfully rather than passively. This might mean leaving thoughtful comments, sending a kind message, or sharing something that reflects your true self. Intentional engagement helps you form genuine connections and avoid mindless scrolling.

5. **End the Week with a Social Media Reflection**

   At the end of the week, reflect on how your mindful social media practices impacted your mood, self-image, or sense of connection. Write down any positive changes or insights you noticed. This reflection reinforces the benefits of mindful social media use and motivates you to keep these habits going.

Final Thought

Mindful social media use is about creating a digital space that reflects your values, supports your well-being, and connects you to people and ideas that uplift you. By approaching social media with intention and authenticity, you reclaim control over your online experience, making it a positive and purposeful extension of your life.

Remember, social media is a tool meant to enhance your life, not to define it. Each time you log in, let your values guide you, your boundaries protect you, and your authenticity shine through. Trust that when you engage mindfully, you bring out the best in yourself—and inspire others to do the same. With mindful social media habits, you can stay true to your unique self, nurture meaningful connections, and build a digital presence that feels grounded, positive, and empowering.

CHAPTER 27

Authenticity in Your Career Path

Many of us grow up with ideas about what a "successful" career looks like, shaped by societal expectations, family, or peer influence. These ideas often create a path defined by "shoulds"—what we should study, where we should work, how much we should earn. But when you build a career based solely on external expectations, it can leave you feeling unfulfilled, disconnected, and even burned out. An authentic career path, by contrast, is one that resonates with your core values, strengths, and passions, allowing you to show up as your true self and find meaning in your work.

Creating a career that aligns with who you are doesn't mean you'll never face challenges or that every day will be easy. It's about choosing a path that feels true, sustainable, and rewarding on a deeper level. This chapter explores how to build a career that reflects your individuality, helps you grow, and makes a positive impact in a way that feels real to you.

How to Build an Authentic Career Path

Building an authentic career requires self-awareness, courage, and a willingness to explore what truly matters to you. Here are steps to help you design a career that feels aligned with your unique self:

1.   **Define Your Core Values**

Start by identifying your core values—the principles that matter most to you. Do you value creativity, helping others, flexibility, continuous learning, or making a social impact? Defining your values allows you to align your career choices with what truly fulfills you and brings meaning to your work.

2.   **Recognize Your Strengths and Talents**

Take an inventory of your natural strengths and talents. Reflect on the skills that come easily to you and the activities that energize you. Building a career around your strengths not only helps you excel but also makes work feel more rewarding, as you're using your unique gifts to make a difference.

3.   **Challenge the "Shoulds" and Rewrite Your Narrative**

Identify any "shoulds" that might be driving your career decisions. These might include expectations from family, societal norms, or ideas of success based on money or prestige. Ask yourself, "Is this path true to who I am, or am I following someone else's idea of success?" Giving yourself permission to let go of "shoulds" allows you to create a career path that reflects your authentic self.

4.   **Explore Career Paths Through Experimentation**

Authentic careers often require exploration. Don't be afraid to experiment with different roles, fields, or projects. Take on freelance work, internships, or side projects that interest you. These experiences help you learn more about what aligns with your values and allow you to refine your path along the way.

5.   **Trust Your Inner Compass**

Your intuition is a valuable guide on your career journey. Notice how different roles, tasks, or environments make you feel. When something aligns, you'll often feel excitement, ease, or a sense of purpose. If something feels draining or inauthentic, it's a signal to reassess. Trust your inner compass as you navigate decisions, knowing it's helping you create a fulfilling path.

Weekly Exercise: The Authentic Career Journal

This week, try using an "Authentic Career Journal" to explore your goals, values, and next steps toward building a career that reflects who you are. This practice encourages self-reflection, clarity, and small but meaningful actions.

1. **Define Your Career Values and Motivations**

   Write down five core values and personal motivations that you want your career to reflect. For example, you might list creativity, flexibility, collaboration, independence, or making a difference. Identifying these values gives you a clear sense of direction and purpose in your career choices.

2. **Reflect on Past Roles or Experiences**

   Think back to past jobs, internships, or volunteer roles that felt fulfilling. What did you enjoy about them? Were you using specific skills or working in a particular environment? Reflecting on these positive experiences helps you see patterns and identify elements you want in your future work.

3. **Challenge a "Should" in Your Career Thinking**

   Write down one "should" that might be holding you back, such as "I should pursue a high-paying job" or "I should work in a stable industry." Reflect on where this belief came from and consider how letting go of it might allow you to explore paths that feel truer to you.

4. **Identify a Small Step Toward an Authentic Career**

   Choose one small, manageable step to take this week that aligns with your values and passions. This could be researching a field of interest, reaching out to someone in a role you admire, updating your resume to reflect your strengths, or taking a class that sparks curiosity. Small steps keep you moving toward a career path that feels right.

5. **Reflect on What You're Learning About Yourself**

At the end of the week, take a few minutes to reflect on what you've learned about yourself. Did any new ideas emerge? Do you feel closer to defining an authentic path? Reflecting on your journey helps you stay aware of your progress and feel grounded in your intentions.

Final Thought

An authentic career isn't built on external measures of success but on choices that align with your unique self. When you let your values, strengths, and passions guide your career path, you create a life of purpose and fulfillment. This journey might not look conventional, and it might not follow a straight line, but it will be deeply rewarding and true to you.

Remember, your career is not just a job or a title—it's an opportunity to contribute to the world in a way that feels meaningful. Trust that you have something valuable to offer and that the right path will reveal itself as you honor your authentic self. Embrace the freedom to define success on your own terms, and know that every step you take brings you closer to a career and life that feel truly aligned.

Let go of the need to "fit in" and instead pursue work that reflects the unique combination of qualities, skills, and dreams that make you who you are. With courage and commitment, you can build a career that honors your true self and allows you to make a difference in a way that's deeply fulfilling.

CHAPTER 28

Embracing Progress Over Perfection

Perfectionism often feels like a constant drive to get everything "just right," a belief that if we can achieve flawlessness, we'll feel secure, respected, or accepted. But instead of bringing peace, perfectionism can lead to procrastination, burnout, self-criticism, and an ongoing sense of "not enough." Letting go of perfectionism doesn't mean settling for mediocrity—it means releasing unrealistic standards and embracing progress as you move forward. It's about choosing growth and fulfillment over an impossible pursuit of flawlessness.

When you replace the need for perfection with a mindset that values progress, you create space for learning, self-compassion, and resilience. This chapter explores how to release perfectionism, shift your focus to progress, and approach your goals with flexibility and grace. By letting go of perfection, you'll find greater satisfaction in your achievements, celebrate small wins, and move through life with more ease and joy.

How to Let Go of Perfectionism and Embrace Progress

Letting go of perfectionism is a gradual practice of self-awareness, self-kindness, and intentional choices. Here are some steps to help you release the need for perfection and focus on the power of progress:

1. **Acknowledge Your Perfectionist Tendencies**

   The first step in letting go of perfectionism is recognizing where it shows up. Do you find yourself redoing work repeatedly, putting off projects until they're "perfect," or avoiding situations where you might make mistakes? Acknowledging these habits helps you understand how perfectionism impacts your life and opens the door to change.

2. **Challenge the Fear of Imperfection**

   Perfectionism is often rooted in a fear of judgment, failure, or loss of control. Ask yourself, "What's the worst that could happen if this isn't perfect?" Most often, the consequences aren't as drastic as they seem. Realizing that imperfections are part of growth helps you let go of rigid standards and accept that mistakes are a natural part of life.

3. **Set "Good Enough" Goals**

   Practice setting goals that are achievable rather than perfect. Instead of aiming for flawless results, aim for meaningful, realistic outcomes. This could mean completing a project by a deadline rather than perfecting every detail or allowing yourself to make mistakes as you learn. "Good enough" goals keep you moving forward without the stress of unattainable standards.

4. **Celebrate Small Wins and Progress**

   Perfectionism can make you overlook small accomplishments, waiting for a perfect result to feel satisfied. Shift your focus by celebrating every step forward, no matter how small. Recognize and appreciate the progress you make, reminding yourself that each step counts and that growth is more important than flawlessness.

5. **Practice Self-Compassion**

   Perfectionism is often fueled by self-criticism. When you make a mistake or fall short of a goal, practice self-compassion by treating yourself with the same kindness you'd offer a friend. Remind yourself that everyone struggles, and that imperfections are a natural part of being human. Self-compassion helps you let go of unrealistic expectations and focus on growth.

Weekly Exercise: The Progress Journal

This week, try using a "Progress Journal" to help you let go of perfectionist habits and focus on meaningful progress. This exercise encourages self-compassion, realistic goal-setting, and small but steady steps forward.

1. **Identify One Area Where You Feel Perfectionist Pressure**

    Begin by identifying one area of your life where you feel the pressure to be perfect, whether it's work, relationships, or personal goals. Write down why you feel the need to achieve perfection in this area, and consider how this pressure affects your well-being.

2. **Set a "Good Enough" Goal**

    Choose a realistic, "good enough" goal related to this area. For example, if you're working on a project, set a goal to complete it within a reasonable timeframe rather than spending endless hours perfecting it. Write down this goal as a reminder to prioritize completion over perfection.

3. **Celebrate Daily Progress**

    Each day, write down one small step you took toward your goal, even if it was just spending five focused minutes on a task. Focusing on small wins helps you recognize that progress is a journey, and each step matters. This practice helps replace the pressure of perfection with the joy of consistent effort.

4. **Challenge One Perfectionist Thought**

    Notice when a perfectionist thought arises, like "I can't make mistakes" or "This has to be flawless." Write down the thought and gently challenge it. Ask yourself, "Is this thought true? Is it helpful?" Reframing these thoughts as "I'm learning as I go" or

"It doesn't have to be perfect to be valuable" helps you rewire your mindset.

5. **Reflect on What You're Learning**
    At the end of the week, reflect on what you learned from focusing on progress over perfection. Did you feel more relaxed or accomplished? Did you make steady progress toward your goal? Reflecting on these insights reinforces the value of letting go of perfection and embracing a growth-focused mindset.

Final Thought

Letting go of perfectionism allows you to live more fully, celebrate progress, and find joy in each step of your journey. When you focus on progress over perfection, you create space for curiosity, growth, and resilience. Rather than striving for an impossible ideal, you honor your own pace and appreciate the value of small, meaningful steps forward.

Remember, perfection is not a prerequisite for happiness or success. Embrace the messy, imperfect process of growth, knowing that each step you take brings you closer to your goals and dreams. Trust that you are enough as you are, and that true fulfillment comes from showing up, doing your best, and finding satisfaction in the journey rather than waiting for a flawless finish.

By releasing the need for perfection, you free yourself to explore, take risks, and move forward with confidence. Embrace progress as a sign of your resilience and strength, and let your path be a reflection of the real, beautifully imperfect journey you're on.

CHAPTER 29

Building Your Own Community

We're all shaped by the people around us, and the right community can be a powerful source of encouragement, inspiration, and accountability. When you're surrounded by people who accept you for who you are and support your growth, it becomes easier to stay authentic, take risks, and pursue your dreams. Finding or building a community that nurtures your true self allows you to connect more deeply with others, feel understood, and have a sense of belonging that uplifts and inspires you.

Building a community doesn't always mean finding a large group of friends or followers; it's about intentionally creating spaces where you can feel safe, seen, and supported. Whether it's a close-knit circle, an online group, or a shared interest club, the communities you create or join should reflect your values and support your growth. This chapter explores how to find, cultivate, and nurture communities that resonate with your authentic self.

How to Build a Community that Supports Your Growth and Authenticity

Creating a community takes intention, vulnerability, and a willingness to reach out. Here are some ways to start building a circle that supports you in becoming your best self:

1. **Identify What You Need from a Community**
   Think about the qualities you want in a community. Are you looking for people who share a passion, encourage self-growth, provide accountability, or simply offer friendship? Knowing what you need helps you find or build a community that aligns with your values and goals, giving you a clear sense of what you're looking for.

2. **Seek Out Shared Interests and Values**
   Communities are often built around shared values, goals, or passions. Consider joining groups, classes, or clubs that center on interests you feel strongly about, whether it's creative hobbies, wellness, career growth, or volunteer work. Shared interests provide a natural foundation for connection and make it easier to bond over common experiences.

3. **Be Open and Vulnerable**
   Authentic communities are created when people are willing to show up as themselves. Share openly, listen, and let others know your true thoughts and feelings. Vulnerability fosters trust and deeper connections, allowing relationships to grow more organically and creating an environment where everyone feels safe to be themselves.

4. **Start Small and Let Connections Grow Naturally**
   Building community doesn't have to happen all at once. Begin by forming a few meaningful connections and letting them deepen over time. Invite a friend to join you at an event, create a small group chat with people who share your goals, or plan regular mee-

tups. Starting small helps cultivate a genuine sense of belonging without the pressure of creating a large circle right away.

5. **Foster a Supportive Environment**

   Be intentional about creating an environment that feels safe and uplifting for everyone involved. Encourage open communication, respect, and kindness within your community. Whether online or in-person, a positive and inclusive atmosphere makes it easier for everyone to feel comfortable sharing, growing, and supporting one another.

Weekly Exercise: The Community Connection Journal

This week, try using a "Community Connection Journal" to explore your current relationships, identify what you need from a community, and take small steps toward building or enhancing one. This exercise encourages reflection, intention, and gentle outreach.

1. **Reflect on Your Current Circle**

   Write down the people or groups you currently connect with regularly. Reflect on whether these relationships feel aligned with your values, support your growth, and encourage your authenticity. Recognizing the strengths and gaps in your existing community helps you decide where to build or invest more.

2. **Identify One Quality You Want in Your Community**

   Think of one quality that's essential in your ideal community—such as positivity, creativity, empathy, or encouragement. Write it down as a reminder to seek out or create spaces that reflect this quality. This intention will guide you in making connections that resonate with your vision of a supportive community.

3. **Take One Step to Reach Out**

   Choose one small way to connect with someone new or deepen an existing connection. This could be inviting a friend for coffee, joining an interest group, or attending a community event. Taking small steps to reach out helps you overcome initial hesitation and brings new opportunities for connection.

4. **Notice How You Feel in Different Environments**
   As you spend time in various social settings, note how each environment makes you feel. Do you feel energized, understood, or inspired? Or do you feel drained or hesitant to share? Noticing these feelings helps you identify which spaces feel authentic and which might not serve your well-being.

5. **Reflect on New Connections and Insights**
   At the end of the week, reflect on any new connections, conversations, or insights you gained. Did you feel a sense of belonging or excitement? Reflecting on these experiences reinforces the importance of community and helps you see the value of intentional relationships.

Final Thought

Building a community that supports your growth and authenticity is one of the most rewarding investments you can make. Surrounding yourself with people who encourage, challenge, and accept you for who you are helps you live a life that feels true, fulfilling, and connected. Remember, community isn't just about numbers; it's about quality, trust, and mutual support.

As you continue to nurture your community, let it be a place where everyone, including yourself, can grow, heal, and thrive. Know that you don't have to do it all at once—small, meaningful steps build the foundation for strong, lasting connections.

Embrace the journey of creating a community that aligns with your values and goals, and trust that the right people will come along as you show up authentically. When you find or build the right community, you'll discover that you're not alone on your path, and that together, you can create something truly special. Let your community be a source of strength, joy, and inspiration as you continue to grow into the fullest, truest version of yourself.

CHAPTER 30

Living True, Day by Day

Living authentically isn't just about making big life changes or deep self-discovery; it's also about showing up as your true self in the small, daily moments. Practicing authenticity each day means making choices that align with who you really are, rather than who you think you're supposed to be. It's about honoring your values, being honest in your interactions, and choosing activities that nourish you. These seemingly small choices add up to a life that feels true and fulfilling, one that reflects your unique path.

This chapter is about cultivating simple, practical habits that help you stay grounded in your authentic self. Living true, day by day, is a journey of consistent self-connection, gentle self-correction, and celebrating the little moments when you feel fully yourself.

Practical Ways to Practice Authenticity Daily

Building a daily habit of authenticity doesn't require big gestures; it's about small, intentional choices that keep you aligned with your values and true to your core. Here are some ways to practice authenticity in your everyday life:

1. **Begin Each Day with Intention**
   Start your day by setting an intention that aligns with your values.

It could be a word, like "courage" or "kindness," or a phrase, such as "I will be true to myself today." Setting an intention grounds you and keeps you focused on what matters, helping you show up authentically in your actions and interactions.

2.　**Check In with Yourself Regularly**

Take small moments throughout the day to check in with yourself. Ask, "How am I feeling right now?" or "Does this feel true to me?" Self-check-ins help you stay connected to your emotions, needs, and boundaries, allowing you to make adjustments if you notice you're straying from your authentic self.

3.　**Make Decisions Based on Values, Not Approval**

When making choices, consider your own values and desires rather than seeking external approval. Ask yourself, "Is this choice aligned with my values?" or "Does this decision feel right to me?" Making decisions based on your own truth, rather than others' expectations, reinforces authenticity in daily life.

4.　**Speak and Act with Honesty**

Authenticity often shows up in the small acts of honesty we practice daily. Whether it's sharing your true opinion, expressing your feelings openly, or setting boundaries kindly, honest communication allows you to show up as you are. Practicing honesty, even in small ways, builds self-trust and fosters deeper, more genuine connections.

5.　**Engage in Activities That Reflect Who You Are**

Each day, make time for activities that genuinely reflect your interests and passions. Whether it's reading, journaling, creating, or moving your body, prioritizing activities that feel true to you helps you stay connected to your authentic self, even in the midst of life's responsibilities.

Weekly Exercise: The Daily Authenticity Tracker

This week, try using a "Daily Authenticity Tracker" to monitor small actions that help you live true to yourself each day. This exercise encourages mindfulness, intention, and a deeper awareness of how you can practice authenticity in daily life.

1. **Set a Daily Intention Aligned with Your Values**

   Each morning, write down an intention that reflects how you want to show up that day. It could be as simple as "I will prioritize honesty" or "I will listen to my needs." Setting a daily intention reinforces your commitment to authenticity and keeps you grounded in your values.

2. **Record One Authentic Action Each Day**

   At the end of each day, jot down one action you took that felt true to your authentic self. It could be setting a boundary, making a choice based on your values, or expressing yourself honestly. Recording these moments helps you appreciate the small steps you're taking toward living authentically.

3. **Reflect on Moments of Misalignment Without Judgment**

   Note any moments when you felt disconnected from your true self. Maybe you said yes when you wanted to say no, or went along with something that didn't feel right. Reflect on these moments with compassion, considering how you might handle similar situations more authentically in the future.

4. **Celebrate Progress Over Perfection**

   Authenticity is a journey, and no one is perfectly aligned with their true self all the time. At the end of the week, take a few minutes to celebrate your progress, however small. Acknowledge the ways you showed up as yourself, and be proud of each step you took toward a more authentic life.

5.   **End Each Day with Gratitude for Your True Self**
Before bed, write down one thing you appreciate about who you are. It could be a quality, a value, or a recent action that felt authentic. Practicing gratitude for your true self helps you build self-acceptance, making it easier to show up authentically each day.

Final Thought

Living true, day by day, is a practice that builds over time. When you make small choices that reflect who you are, you create a life that feels aligned, fulfilling, and real. Authenticity isn't a destination; it's a journey of self-connection, self-compassion, and continuous growth. Each day is an opportunity to reconnect with your core values and bring your unique self into the world.

Remember, living authentically doesn't mean being perfect; it means being present and honest with yourself in each moment. Trust that each choice to honor your true self, no matter how small, is a step toward a life that feels genuinely aligned with who you are. Embrace the freedom that comes with authenticity, and let it guide you to a life that feels purposeful, joyful, and undeniably you.

By living true, day by day, you build a foundation of authenticity that becomes the heart of your journey. Each moment, each choice, and each step forward is a reflection of the beautiful, unique individual that you are. Embrace your path with courage and gratitude, and know that the life you're creating, one day at a time, is an expression of your truest self.

EMBRACING THE LIFELONG PATH OF SELF-DISCOVERY

As you come to the end of this book, remember that your journey of self-discovery is only just beginning. Living authentically and honoring your true self isn't a one-time achievement or a final destination; it's a lifelong path of learning, growing, and deepening your connection to who you are. There is no "perfect" version of yourself waiting to be unlocked—only layers of understanding, acceptance, and wisdom that reveal themselves over time.

Self-discovery is not about arriving fully formed, but about giving yourself the freedom to evolve. It's about allowing yourself the space to grow and change, letting go of the need to have it all figured out. This journey is as much about learning to love yourself in moments of uncertainty as it is about celebrating your progress along the way.

Honoring Who You Are, Day by Day

Living authentically means showing up for yourself each day, making choices that reflect your values, and staying true to what feels right for you. Some days, this will feel natural and effortless; on others, it might be challenging. But each choice you make to honor your true self is a step closer to the life you're meant to lead. Remember that authenticity doesn't mean getting it "right" all the time—it means approaching each day with openness and curiosity, allowing yourself to learn and grow from each experience.

As you continue on this path, know that you have the strength to navigate both the beautiful and challenging moments. Keep asking questions, keep exploring, and give yourself permission to change your mind as you gain new insights. The journey of becoming is a dynamic, unfolding process, one that brings you closer to the core of who you are as you discover new aspects of yourself.

Choosing Authenticity Every Day

Living authentically is a choice you get to make every day. It's the decision to listen to your intuition, to honor your unique perspective, and to trust that your path is valid, even if it looks different from anyone else's. The journey may sometimes feel uncertain, but it's precisely this uncertainty that gives life its richness. Each choice to be true to yourself, each step taken with integrity, strengthens your sense of purpose and connection to the world around you.

Remember that there is no end to becoming. The beauty of self-discovery lies in its endless potential, in the joy of uncovering more of yourself as you continue forward. Embrace the journey with compassion, patience, and courage. Trust that by choosing authenticity, you are creating a life that's not only meaningful but also deeply fulfilling.

Keep Going, Stay Curious, and Embrace the Journey

As you move forward, keep going with a heart full of curiosity and openness. Allow yourself to be surprised by where this path of self-discovery takes you. There will be twists and turns, triumphs and setbacks, but through it all, remember that this journey is yours to shape and explore. You don't need to have all the answers to be on the right path; all you need is the willingness to be true to yourself, one day at a time.

Embrace the journey of becoming as the beautiful, lifelong process that it is. Continue to honor who you are, trust in your growth, and celebrate the unique person you're becoming. The choice to live authentically is yours to make every single day—may you make it with courage, love, and the knowledge that each step brings you closer to the fullest, truest version of you.